Wakeful Words

CLASSICAL RHETORICAL TECHNIQUES IN LITERATURE

> "Hence sprung an artless and unlaboured harmony which seems the natural heritage of Elizabethan poets, whereas such harmony as is attained by modern authors frequently betrays a painful excess of art.... We may perhaps claim some superiority in completeness and perspicuity for modern English, but if we were to appeal on this ground to the shade of Shakespeare in the words of Antonio in the *Tempest,*—'Do you not hear us speak?' we might fairly be crushed with the reply of Sebastian—'I do; and surely it is a sleepy language.'"
>
> —E. A. Abbott, *A Shakespearean Grammar*
> (London and New York: Macmillan and Co., 1870)

A companion to the literature of Classical Conversations

compiled and edited by Jen Greenholt

Classical Conversations, *Wakeful Words*
©2016 Classical Conversations® MultiMedia, Inc. All rights reserved.

Published by Classical Conversations® MultiMedia
P.O. Box 909
West End, NC 27376
www.ClassicalConversations.com | www.ClassicalConversationsBooks.com

Cover design by Classical Conversations.

All Scripture quotations, unless otherwise noted, are taken from the *Holy Bible, New International Version®. NIV®*. Copyright © 1984, by International Bible Society. Used by permission of Zondervan. All rights reserved. Scripture verses marked KJV are from the King James Version of the Bible.

Printed in the United States of America.
All rights reserved. No part of this publication may be reproduced, stored in a retrieval system, or transmitted in any form by any means, electronic, mechanical, photocopy, recording, or otherwise, without prior permission of the author, except as provided by USA copyright law.

ISBN 978-0-9965660-3-2

Honoring copyright: it is a matter of integrity!
Classical Conversations works diligently to keep costs down and provide helpful resources for your family's home school. This book is copyrighted, which means that unauthorized reproduction or sharing of the pages is prohibited. This includes sharing copies with other families or groups, even within your own community. Rather, encourage your friends who would like this resource to honor copyright and invest by subscribing to CC Connected for this and other resources. Permission is granted to make copies within your own home for your family.

Table of Contents

Introduction 5

Terms and Definitions 6

Examples from Challenge A Literature 9

Examples from Challenge B Literature 23

Examples from Challenge I Literature 33

Examples from Challenge II Literature 47

Examples from Challenge III Literature 61

Examples from Challenge IV Literature 73

Examples from the Bible 87

Introduction

"Friends, Romans, countrymen—lend me your ears!"

In ancient Rome many great orators walked the Roman Forum. To stand out, an orator had to acquire and employ an extensive tool kit of tropes, schemes, and devices that he used to appeal not only to his audience's ears but also to the audience's minds and memories. To the Romans, rhetoric was a particular art form and a prerequisite for being a persuasive, influential leader. European nobles of the Renaissance period admired the structure and order of Greek and Roman civilization and sought to recreate it, so they tried to mimic some elements of ancient education and art, including rhetorical study. As a result, classical rhetoric saw a revival among the courts of France, Spain, England, and other nations of Western Europe.

Although classical rhetoric and its tool kit are no longer a required course of study for most aspiring leaders and intellectuals, writers and speakers today use many of the same classical techniques once prominent in ancient Rome. Think of Martin Luther King, Jr.'s famous "I Have a Dream" speech. His refrain, "I have a dream," is an example of **anaphora**. He uses **litotes** when he says, "I am not unmindful that some of you have come here out of great trials and tribulations." He also uses **parallelism**, **polysyndeton**, **metaphors**, and **personification**, terms that this document will help you to recognize.

Learning to see these devices in the writing of others will not only make you a better reader but will also prepare you to become a stronger, more persuasive writer and speaker. You will have new access to ancient techniques that appeal to the eyes, the ears, the mind, and ultimately, the heart. Broadly speaking, most classical rhetorical techniques can be divided into two categories:

Schemes (S) — writing devices that deal with form, sounds, or word order and appeal to the senses.

Tropes (T) — writing devices that deal with images, ideas, or word meanings and appeal to the mind (memory or imagination).

This selection of rhetorical devices, although not comprehensive, will introduce you to some of the most commonly used techniques in classical rhetoric. First, each term is defined. Next, examples are presented from classic writings and literature. When you finish reading, you should begin to notice these devices in other books you read on your own.

Keep in mind, the goal of this project is not to give you an exhaustive catalog of every literary trope or scheme used in every work of literature you will ever study; rather, it is to cultivate in you the practice of recognizing and naming these devices. Your eyes should pause, and you should begin to ask yourself the questions, "Why is this here? What purpose does it serve? How does it enhance or detract from (this book / this poem / my own writing)?" When you can do that consistently, you will have added another valuable instrument to your reader and writer's tool kit.

See what happened there? That's called a metaphor. To find out more, keep reading.

Terms and Definitions

Alliteration — Latin, *ad-* (to) + *littera* (letter)

Repetition of initial consonant sounds or vowel sounds in close proximity. This technique was used instead of or alongside rhyming in Old and Middle English poetry. (S)

When the <u>w</u>inter <u>w</u>inds blew <u>w</u>hite snow across the <u>w</u>ater, <u>w</u>e <u>w</u>ent <u>w</u>est.

Allusion — Latin, *ad-* (to) + *ludere* (to play)

An indirect reference to another literary work or to a historical figure or event. Sometimes the reference is to a character; other times it refers to a famous line or quotation. (T)

Give me liberty, or—well, really, just give me liberty. I dislike the alternative.

Anaphora — Greek, *ana-* (back) + *pherein* (to bear)

Repetition of a word or a phrase at the beginning of subsequent clauses, lines, or sentences. (S)

<u>We call beauty</u> strange. <u>We call beauty</u> irrational. <u>We call beauty</u> unapproachable.

Antithesis — Greek, *anti-* (against) + *tithenai* (to place)

Statement of a proposition and its opposite in close proximity. (S)

<u>It was the hottest summer</u> she had ever seen, and at the same time <u>it was the coldest</u>.

Apostrophe — Greek, *apo-* (from) + *strephein* (to turn)

A form of address directed to an invisible being, an abstract concept, or an absent or nonexistent person. Apostrophe is often used in invocations. (T)

<u>Oh, Time!</u> If only I had more time.

Assonance — Latin, *ad-* (to) + *sonare* (to sound)

Repetition of vowel sounds or patterns of vowel sounds in the final stressed syllable of a line. Assonance is not true rhyme because the associated consonants differ. (S)

She walked to the w<u>i</u>ndow / where the birds came to s<u>i</u>ng.

Asyndeton — Greek, *a-* (not) + *syndein* (to bind together)

A series of clauses, typically joined by coordinating conjunctions, in which the conjunctions are removed to create a condensed, emphatic sentence. Asyndeton refers to a lack of connection within the sentence. (T)

We bought candy, we sailed boats, we played on swing sets. We did everything.

Chiasmus — Greek, *khiazein* (to mark with an "x")

From the Greek letter *chi* (X), a group of words or sounds presented and then repeated in reverse. Chiasmus may refer to a combination of sounds, the order of a sentence's parts of speech, or a combination of words. (S)

My son's face rested on my mind as my hand rested on the little boy's face.

Consonance — Latin, *com-* (with) + *sonare* (to sound)

Repetition of final consonant sounds, typically at the end of a line of verse. Consonance differs from rhyme in that the preceding vowel sounds are not the same. (S)

A hu<u>sh</u> fell over the room as the po<u>sh</u> knight announced his wi<u>sh</u>.

Epistrophe — Greek, *epi-* (upon) + *strophe* (a turning)

Repetition of words or phrases at the end of successive stanzas, clauses, lines, or sentences. (S)

He walked into <u>the garden</u>. He bent to dig in <u>the garden</u>. He rested in <u>the garden</u>.

Foreshadowing — Old English, *fore-* (before) + *sceadwe* (shadow)

The use of textual clues (in dialogue or description) to predict a later event or outcome. Some foreshadowing is subtle and difficult to recognize except in retrospect, while some is explicitly used to create suspense. (T)

As the king prepared to enter battle, dark storm clouds gathered on the horizon. (Implied: this battle will not end well for the king.)

Terms and Definitions

Hyperbole — Greek, *hyper-* (beyond) + *bole* (a throwing)

Exaggeration for literary effect, either humor or emphasis. (T)

The green box in front of them was the biggest one in the whole world!

Imagery — Latin, *imago* (copy, picture)

Use of vivid, specific, and descriptive language that evokes a strong image or appeals to the senses. Imagery often uses familiar comparisons to give shape to a new or unfamiliar concept. (T)

She gripped the rough bars of her cell and watched through the iron fence as a bird took flight through the damp mist.

Litotes — Greek, *litos* (smooth, plain)

A form of understatement that consists of negating the idea's opposite. (T)

Trust me, I am not unaware of your plight.

Metaphor — Greek, *meta-* (across) + *pherein* (to carry)

An implicit comparison between two unlike things, or between a character or event and a broader theme, concept, or idea. (T)

The wind carved a serrated path through the snow. (Implied: wind = knife)

Metonymy — Greek, *meta-* (change) + *onoma* (name)

Use of an object closely associated with an idea to represent the idea itself. Metonymy is distinct from synecdoche because the word used to represent the idea is not necessarily part of what it references. (T)

The soldiers knew the threat he posed to the Crown. (Implied: crown = kingdom)

Onomatopoeia — Greek, *onoma-* (name) + *poiein* (to make)

A word created to represent a specific sound. The word is pronounced in such a way that it mimics the meaning of the word. More generally, onomatopoeia can refer to the way the overall sound of a poem reflects its meaning. (T)

The bees buzzed angrily around the honeysuckle.

Parallelism — Greek, *para-* (beside) + *allos* (other)

An arrangement in which two or more elements of equal importance are arranged using similar phrasing or sentence structure. Parallelism may apply to verb forms, clauses, or entire sentences. (S)

She walked to the parking lot, drove to the airport, and then ran to the terminal.

Personification — Latin, *persona-* (person) + *facere* (to make)

Attribution of human characteristics to an inanimate object or non-human entity. (T)

The alarm clock yelled at her from across the darkened bedroom.

Polysyndeton — Greek, *poly-* (many) + *syndein* (to bind together)

A series of clauses with coordinating conjunctions preceding each item, not just the final item in the series, as is typical. (S)

He stared at the crushed car, and the mangled trees, and the decimated house.

Rhyme — Greek, *rhythmos* (measured time)

Two words with the same final consonant and/or vowel sound. Imperfect rhymes, also called near rhymes, may have the same vowel sound but a different final consonant (assonance), or the same concluding consonant but a different vowel sound (consonance). Rhymes can occur in the middle as well as at the end of a line. (S)

When the stars began to trace the sky / the bats began to fly.

Simile — Latin, *simile* (a like thing)

An explicit comparison, signified by the words "like," "as," or "than." (T)

The book was rough and red like an oversized brick.

Synecdoche — Greek, *syn-* (with) + *ek* (out) + *dekhesthai* (to receive)

Substitution of part of an object for the whole, or vice versa. Synecdoche is a more specific form of metonymy. (T)

Four hooves trotted by her hiding place, and she held her breath. (Implied: four hooves = horse)

Now that you have learned the names of some of the most common rhetorical techniques, go back and read the introduction again. See how many rhetorical devices you can find and identify. You'll be amazed at what your eyes ignored before you knew where to look. When you are ready, you can move on to study examples found in classic writings, both ancient and modern.

EXAMPLES FROM

Challenge A

LITERATURE

Examples from Challenge A Literature

These examples are drawn from notable works of children's literature, many of which are Newbery Medal winners. Unlike formal poetry, which emphasizes deliberate use of rhetorical techniques, prose writing tends to use these devices in subtler ways. The author may not even be aware that he or she is using asyndeton or alliteration, but in the course of trying to create a specific tone and style, he or she unwittingly makes use of the rhetorician's tool kit. As a conscientious reader and a writer-in-training, your appreciation for these books will become richer as you become more aware of the subtle and beautiful ways the authors use language to tell a story.

All of these classic books are available in multiple editions, so unless you are using the same edition as the one cited in the bibliography, page numbers may not match precisely.

Alliteration

- *The Door in the Wall*, "<u>W</u>hen he <u>w</u>as fed, Brother Luke, who had talked quietly the <u>w</u>hile, fetched <u>w</u>ater in a basin, <u>w</u>ashed him, and in other <u>w</u>ays made him comfortable" (p. 15).

  The repeated consonant sound "w" creates alliteration in this scene. The sound is gentle rather than harsh and matches Brother Luke's treatment of Robin.

- *The Bronze Bow*, "'But at least you don't have to look at them. There's a for<u>tr</u>ess at Capernaum. I'll have to watch them all the time, <u>str</u>utting around the <u>str</u>eets'" (p. 9).

  Read this selection aloud. In this example of alliteration, repeating the consonant sound "str," you can almost hear the snarl in Joel's voice.

- *The Secret Garden*, "He showed her ten thousand new green <u>p</u>oints <u>p</u>ushing through the mould" (p. 204).

  The letter "p" makes a sharp, explosive sound, releasing a puff of air when you pronounce it. In this way, the sound of the alliterative phrase "points pushing" mirrors the appearance of sprouts emerging from the ground.

- *A Gathering of Days*, "We only <u>p</u>aused but once on the way, and that to <u>p</u>ick some <u>p</u>ods and grasses close by the side of the road" (p. 17).

Sometimes an author uses alliteration for a specific purpose, but sometimes the device simply shows variety and adds richness and beauty to the writing. A judicious reader should consider what purpose the rhetorical device serves, and whether it adds to or detracts from the writing. A judicious writer, then, makes the same decision before including rhetorical flourishes in his or her prose.

Allusion

- *Number the Stars*, "'Save a little from what?' Annemarie asked, spooning oatmeal into a flowered bowl. 'Don't tell me the soldiers try to—what's the word? —<u>*relocate*</u> butter, too?'" (p. 68).

  An allusion subtly prompts the reader to remember something that was mentioned earlier in the book or in another context (e.g., another work of literature, a historical event, or a work of art). Here, in an attempt to find humor in an ugly situation, Annemarie alludes to her father's explanation that the German soldiers want to arrest and relocate all the Danish Jews. She does not mention the Jews by name, but the key word "relocate," emphasized in italics, reminds readers that this concept has appeared before in a different context.

- *The Secret Garden*, "'Shall they, <u>Mr. Rajah</u>!' Mary said fiercely. 'They may drag me in but they can't make me talk when they get me here'" (p. 217).

  When Mary calls Colin "Mr. Rajah," she is referring to a story she had told earlier about an Indian rajah who ordered around his subjects in an imperious and haughty manner. She does not explain her allusion, but readers are expected to remember this exchange and understand that Mary is accusing Colin of being spoiled and haughty.

Anaphora

- *Amos Fortune, Free Man*, "They heard him late that night singing in the darkness of the tannery—
    '<u>You got to cross</u> that river Jordan,
    <u>You got to cross</u> it for yourself;
    O there can't nobody cross it for you,
    <u>You got to cross</u> it for yourself'" (p. 63).

Many songs use anaphora to reiterate an important message or link similar ideas together. In this example, Amos's song expresses his feeling of discouragement about his search for his sister. He is facing a river that he has to cross alone.

- *The Secret Garden*, "'He has flown over the wall!' Mary cried out, watching him. '<u>He has flown</u> into the orchard—<u>he has flown</u> across the other wall—into the garden where there is no door!'" (p. 53).

Mary's repetition of the initial phrase "he has flown" gives readers the impression that she is narrating the robin's actions play by play, with pauses in between. The use of anaphora increases the reader's anticipation for what will come next.

Antithesis

- *Amos Fortune, Free Man*, "<u>The slavers ate well and drank freely</u>. Then, while the sun was at its highest, pouring fierce heat upon the land, they crept under crudely constructed shelters of wide palm leaves and slept. <u>No one took any thought of the At-mun-shi</u>. Under the rain of heat they waited patiently, each one knowing that a rain of fire would be his if he moved" (pp. 15–16).

Antithesis creates tension for the reader. The slavers' ease and comfort stands in sharp contrast to the slaves' misery. If you removed the first half of this passage and only told what happened to the slaves, the scene would have a milder effect because readers might assume that the slavers were enduring similar physical hardship in the African heat.

- *The Lion, the Witch and the Wardrobe*, "'But how could it be true, sir?' said Peter.
    'Why do you say that?' asked the Professor.
    'Well, for one thing,' said Peter, 'if it was real why doesn't everyone find this country every time they go to the wardrobe? I mean, <u>there was nothing there when we looked</u>; even Lucy didn't pretend there was.'
    'What has that to do with it?' said the Professor.
    'Well, sir, <u>if things are real, they're there all the time</u>.'
    'Are they?' said the Professor; and Peter did not know quite what to say" (p. 49).

Peter identifies what are, to him, two contradictory ideas. First, real things do not disappear at whim. Second, Lucy is usually a truthful person, but she insists that she has been to a real place that is not always visible. Peter's conclusion is that Lucy is either lying or mad, but the Professor points out a third possibility: Peter's first premise was flawed. As the children discover, some real places are capable of disappearing and reappearing under specific circumstances.

Apostrophe

- *The Bronze Bow*, "'Daniel!' he choked. 'I will take the oath too! <u>Before heaven</u>, I will avenge your father! I swear it! I will fight them as long as I live!'" (p. 84).

Imagine, during this scene, that Joel points up to the ceiling when he says, "Before heaven." Examples of apostrophe could often be accompanied by this gesture, because apostrophe invokes something above or outside the people actually present. Here, Joel swears "before heaven," meaning "before God," who is not physically present.

- *The Secret Garden*, "'I never knowed how tha' got so thick wi' me. If it hadna' been for th' robin—<u>Drat him</u>—'" (p. 286).

In Ben Weatherstaff's anger, he says of the robin, "Drat him," which could be rephrased as "may he be 'dratted.'" It has the form of a mild curse, another form of apostrophe.

- *Carry On, Mr. Bowditch*, "He could almost hear Lizza's whisper again: 'If you squinch your eyes, Nat, it looks exactly like flowers—almost—doesn't it?'

Nat clenched his hands and stared at the water until it blurred. He looked up at the sky. The stars blurred, too. '<u>I don't see any help in the stars! Not now!</u>'" (p. 77).

Nat is addressing his sister, who has recently died, and responding to a statement she had made years ago. He does not expect her to respond, but he speaks as though she were still alive.

- *Crispin: The Cross of Lead*, "Instead, I bowed my head in prayer: '<u>O Great and Giving Jesus</u>, I, who have no name, who am nothing, who do not know what to do, who am all alone in Thy world, I, who am full of sin, I implore Thy blessed help, or I'm undone'" (p. 25).

Not all forms of apostrophe appeal to a non-existent or absent entity. In literature, prayer is another form of apostrophe because it appeals to a higher, invisible being for blessing and support. Like other uses of apostrophe, a prayer points the reader's eyes higher than the physical setting of the story.

Assonance

- *The Bronze Bow*, "Daniel closed his t<u>ee</u>th on a familiar oath. 'I curse the air they br<u>ea</u>the,' he muttered.

'I env<u>y</u> you,' said Joel. 'Up h<u>e</u>re you're fr<u>ee</u>'" (p. 9).

This passage demonstrates assonance, repeating the long "e" vowel sound. You can pronounce this sound with your teeth clenched in anger, as Joel's and Daniel's might have been.

Asyndeton

- *Number the Stars*, "All of those things, those sources of pride—<u>the candlesticks, the books, the daydreams of theater</u>—had been left behind in Copenhagen" (pp. 93–94).

The list could read, "the candlesticks, the books, and the daydreams of theater." By leaving out the final coordinating conjunction that grammar would demand, the author gives the reader a sense that the list is not complete; the Rosens have left behind many things from their past life, not just these three.

- *Amos Fortune, Free Man*, "Desolate, <u>deprived of their youth, their strength, their leadership</u>, what were a handful of old people and children to do in the jungle?" (pp. 11–12).

In a scene like this one, asyndeton can emphasize suffering or loss. The sentence feels unbalanced and incomplete, as if the narrator struggles to finish his thought or express it properly. Someone who has been struck by tragedy may find it difficult to speak coherently or in grammatically correct sentences. Asyndeton can convey that same tone in a passage of writing.

Chiasmus

- *Amos Fortune, Free Man*, "'I mean that <u>we've made others slaves</u> readily enough but <u>we'll be slaves</u> ourselves if we don't keep watch'" (p. 64).

Mr. Richardson notices the similarity of the slaves' plight under their white masters and that of the American colonists under the British. The construction of his sentence shows that similarity. The first half of the sentence consists of S (we) + V (have made) + DO (others) + PN (slaves). The second half of the sentence almost exactly reverses it by using an implied passive verb instead of an active one: S (we) + V (will be [made]) + PN (slaves). When Mr. Richardson recognizes that both are examples of injustice, he finally takes action to give Amos his freedom.

- *The Secret Garden*, "'<u>People never like me and I never like people</u>,' she thought" (pp. 46–47).

The chiasmus here is more apparent than in the previous example. Mary directly inverts the first statement in the second one: S (people) + V (never like) + DO (me) becomes S (I) + V (never like) + DO (people).

Consonance

- *Number the Stars*, "His eyes turned to the page he had opened at random, and he began to read in a strong voice.

    O praise the <u>Lord</u>.
    How good it is to sing psalms to our <u>God</u>!
    How pleasant to praise <u>him</u>!
    The Lord is rebuilding <u>Jerusalem</u>…" (p. 86).

The psalm that Peter chooses to read contains two examples of consonance. Both "Lord" and "God" have the same final consonant sound but different preceding vowel sounds. Similarly, "him" and "Jerusalem" share a final consonant but differ in their final vowels.

Epistrophe

- *The Secret Garden*, "'He's made up his mind to make friends <u>with thee</u>,' replied Ben. 'Dang me if he hasn't took a fancy <u>to thee</u>.'

'To me?' said Mary, and she moved toward the little tree softly and looked up.

'Would you make friends <u>with me</u>?' she said to the robin just as if she was speaking to a person" (p. 52).

This exchange demonstrates both chiasmus and epistrophe as Mary echoes Ben's words to the robin. Repeating the phrase "to/with thee/me" emphasizes her disbelief that the bird would find her a suitable friend. The reader can sense Mary's insecurity more clearly as a result.

Foreshadowing

- *The Bronze Bow*, "Underneath the scarf the long yellow hair was always combed and carefully arranged. Was it the work in the little garden that had brought a faint flush to [Leah's] pale cheeks?" (p. 142).

Daniel passes quickly over this observation, and the reader may be tempted to do the same. Only later in the novel do we discover that this fact foreshadows later discoveries. This is an example of subtle foreshadowing—the reader is given no more information than the character receives in the moment.

- *The Door in the Wall*, "She had drawn Robin to her and had turned away so he would not see her tears. <u>Little did she know how much Robin would need her!</u>

"For the very next day he had become ill and unable to move his legs" (p. 8).

This passage shows more explicit foreshadowing, which is explained in the very next sentence. The author satisfies the reader's curiosity almost immediately, allowing us to move ahead without distraction.

Hyperbole

- *Amos Fortune, Free Man*, "They were alone in the kitchen and she put her head on his shoulder and sobbed <u>as if the tears she had not wept for twenty years were coming at last</u>" (p. 79).

No one can store tears for twenty years, but the author uses this exaggeration as a way to help the reader understand the depth of Lydia's emotion when she talks about her trials on the Middle Passage.

- *Carry On, Mr. Bowditch*, "'I don't know why, but David seems to think you're quite a man! He said if I ever had trouble with you, <u>I'd swing from a yardarm</u>!'" (p. 72).

In the previous scene, Nat convinces his sister Mary that she loves David enough to take the risk of marrying a sailor. In this exchange, Mary knows that her new husband would not actually hang her from the yardarm of a ship, but she wants to make a point about how much David appreciates Nat's advocacy on his behalf, so she exaggerates.

Imagery

- *The Magician's Nephew*, "The <u>stone</u> of which everything was built <u>seemed to be red</u>, but that might only be because of the <u>curious light</u>. It was obviously very old. Many of the <u>flat stones</u> that paved the courtyard had <u>cracks</u> across them. None of them fitted closely together and the <u>sharp corners were all worn off</u>. One of the <u>arched doorways</u> was half filled up with rubble" (p. 45).

In part, this passage describes the world that Digory and Polly have entered. The author is describing concrete features of the world. At the same time, however, he is giving his characters and the reader a sense of what the world is like. He uses these concrete images of broken stone and debris to show that this is an old, damaged world with an ominous quality. The story goes on to confirm this initial impression.

- *The Lion, the Witch and the Wardrobe*, "'Didn't I tell you,' answered Mr. Beaver, 'that she'd made it always winter and never Christmas? Didn't I tell you? Well, just come and see!'

And then they were all at the top and did see.

It *was* a <u>sledge</u>, and it was <u>reindeer with bells on their harness</u>. But they were <u>far bigger than the Witch's reindeer</u>, and they were not white but <u>brown</u>. And on the sledge sat <u>a person whom everyone knew</u> the moment they set eyes on him" (p. 106).

One symbol of the Witch's power in Narnia is her ability to prevent Christmas from coming. When the Beavers and the children meet Father Christmas, he serves as a symbol of the Witch's weakening control over Narnia. Rather than simply telling his readers that the witch's power is waning, the author uses the rich, detailed imagery of Christmas to demonstrate this fact to the children as well as to his readers.

Litotes

- *The Secret Garden*, "Mary said nothing at all, and Mrs. Medlock looked rather discomfited by her apparent indifference, but, after taking a breath, she went on. '<u>Not but</u> that it's a grand big place in a gloomy way, and Mr. Craven's proud of it in his way—and that's gloomy enough, too'" (p. 18).

Mrs. Medlock's phrasing is part of her Yorkshire accent, so it differs from other examples of litotes you may see. If you were to expand the implied sentence, however, it might read, "Not that it is not a grand big place." The two negatives ("not" and "but" or "not" and "not") cancel out one another, so the sentence actually means, "It is a grand big place in a gloomy way." Giving Mrs. Medlock a strong accent allows the author to distinguish her speech from that of other characters.

Metaphor

- *The Door in the Wall*, "Then Robin heard the big fellow say, 'By my beard, <u>the birds have flown</u>!'" (p. 61).

The thief is not referring to a literal flight of birds; he is using the metaphor of birds flying out of a cage to explain that Robin and the monks have escaped from their trap.

- *Amos Fortune, Free Man*, "Where the <u>great bird</u> in whose <u>belly</u> they lay would bear them he did not know" (p. 25).

The sails on a ship resemble the wings of a bird, and At-mun carries the metaphor further by identifying the ship's hold with the belly of a bird of prey. This metaphor reflects At-mun's experiences; he is more familiar with birds than with oceangoing ships. Notice the difference between this metaphor and a simile: At-mun never refers to it as a ship, and the author does not directly link "ship" and "bird." She leaves that task up to the reader.

- *The Lion, the Witch and the Wardrobe*, "Then, when he saw all the other creatures start forward and heard Aslan say with a wave of his paw, 'Back! <u>Let the Prince win his spurs</u>,' he did understand, and set off running as hard as he could to the pavilion" (p. 130).

Peter does not need to acquire a physical pair of spurs. Aslan's metaphor may be a familiar one even to modern readers who do not know its origin. The metaphor refers to the fact that in medieval times, when a man became a full-fledged knight, he was awarded a pair of gilded spurs. "Winning one's spurs" can then be understood to mean proving one's maturity or readiness for combat. Aslan is saying that Peter needs to kill the wolf in order to prove that he is ready to be a prince.

- *Crispin: The Cross of Lead*, "These confessions were numerous, since I had become convinced that there was some sin <u>embedded</u> in me, a sin I was desperate <u>to root out</u>" (p. 13).

The boy does not make an explicit comparison using "like" or "as," but he talks about his unknown sin as though it were a thorn in his foot or a weed in a garden. Readers who have never felt this way about a sin may have experienced weeding a garden or removing a thorn. As a result of this metaphor, they are better able to understand how difficult it seems for the boy to find and purge the sin.

Metonymy

- *Amos Fortune, Free Man*, "The struggling colonies had been <u>bound together by words on a parchment</u>, words that said 'All men are created equal…'" (p. 76).

The colonies were not literally tied together by words on a parchment. The Declaration of Independence, rather, stood in for their collective desire to be free. It became associated with the colonists' determination and boldness.

- *Carry On, Mr. Bowditch*, "Zack sidled to the door before he fired his parting shot. 'Thanks to God, maybe. <u>No thanks to *books*</u>!' And he scuttled out" (p. 216).

The irate man is not referring to all books. The reader knows from context that he is talking specifically about sailing by mathematical charts rather than by traditional instruments of navigation. This is known as "sailing by the book." Readers know that a book cannot physically sail a ship. Instead, "the book" stands in for the mathematical calculations Nat and others like him use to determine their ships' courses.

- *The Lion, the Witch and the Wardrobe*, "She would have known that when a willing victim who had committed no treachery was killed in a traitor's stead, the Table would crack and Death itself would start working backward" (p. 163).

The Stone Table is an altar where the Witch has the right to sacrifice traitors. The Deep Magic, which governs all of Narnia, is written on the table, but the table is merely a physical object that represents Narnia's laws. When the table cracks in this scene, the broken stone is symbolic of Aslan's fulfillment of the law, rendering the table unnecessary.

Onomatopoeia

- *The Door in the Wall*, "Sometimes there were long silences, when he heard nothing but the mewing of the cat Millicent, or the squeaking of a mouse she had caught" (p. 19).

The sound a cat makes is very similar to the pronunciation of the word "mew." Likewise, it is difficult to pronounce the word "squeak" without making a sound like that of a mouse. Here, onomatopoeia helps readers imagine the sounds Robin heard in the quiet cell.

- *Number the Stars*, "Inside the house, Mama scrubbed and dusted, tsk-tsking at Uncle Henrik's untidy housekeeping" (p. 70).

The word "tsk" does not have a particular meaning, but it mimics the sound someone might make to express disdain or disapproval.

- *The Lion, the Witch and the Wardrobe*, "It was the noise of running water. All round them, though out of sight, there were streams, chattering, murmuring, bubbling, splashing and even (in the distance) roaring" (p. 118).

A clue to the author's need for onomatopoeia in this passage is the phrase "out of sight." Edmund cannot see the water, and (for obvious reasons) neither can the reader. Instead, the author makes the invisible spring thaw vivid using another sense: hearing. Each word he uses to describe the flowing water sounds like its meaning. Say the words aloud to see for yourself.

- *Crispin: The Cross of Lead*, "A steady, hissing rain had turned the ground to clinging mud" (p. 1).

When you say the word "hiss," you imitate the sound of a hissing snake. Describing the rain as hissing rather than dripping makes this scene more vivid, and it adds an ominous tone that matches the action of the scene.

Parallelism

- *The Door in the Wall*, "He loved the smell of the wood he was whittling, even the acrid smell of the oak that Brother Matthew was working. He liked the sharp whistle of the plane as it slid over the board, and the ringing sound of the chisel on stone from the mason's shed" (pp. 27–28).

These two sentences are parallel on multiple levels. In terms of structure, both begin with an independent clause in the sentence pattern S-V*t*-DO with a prepositional phrase modifying the direct object. In terms of content, each sentence deals with one of the five senses as Robin experiences it while he is carving.

- *The Magician's Nephew*, "The stuff in the yellow rings had the power of drawing you into the wood; it was stuff that wanted to get back to its own place, the in-between place. But the stuff in the green rings is stuff that is trying to get out of its own place; so that a green ring would take you out of the wood into a world" (p. 42).

The parallelism in this passage is on the level of content. As a storyteller, the author uses two objects (rings) with comparable powers but opposite effects to move his story forward.

- *Crispin: The Cross of Lead*, "No one knelt. They simply stared. As they had shunned my mother in life, so they shunned her now" (p. 2).

This is an example of parallelism on the level of the sentence as well as the level of content. For the reader, this simple statement, made very early in the book, contains a wealth of information. The narrator points out that the villagers are consistent in their treatment of his mother, but their response to the woman's death seems harsh. In this way, without being heavy-handed, the device encourages the reader to wonder what the boy's mother could have possibly done to deserve being shunned in life and death.

Personification

- *The Door in the Wall*, "<u>Hunger bit at his empty stomach</u>. He was hungry enough now to have eaten the porridge Ellen had brought him" (p. 12).

Robin describes hunger (a physical sensation) as though it were a person with sharp teeth inside of him, gnawing at his belly. This is a common way to personify hunger.

- *Amos Fortune, Free Man*, "Blossoms of brilliant hue were twice beautiful <u>as they found their reflections in the water</u>. All along the way <u>the land cried out</u> the year's new growth" (p. 17).

The author uses personification to express how verdant and lush the surrounding land is. Personification makes it seem that the flowers are looking at themselves in a mirror and the land is talking about the new greenery emerging. This device demonstrates At-mun's close relationship to his country and his sorrow at leaving it.

- *A Gathering of Days*, "Father says that when he is done with the spindled maple wood chair he'll not make a candle-stand after all, but rather another matching chair <u>to keep it company</u>. 'Would not a chair want that,' he jokes, 'same as a mortal being?'" (p. 48).

This is an example of using literary devices to create humor. Father acknowledges by his laughter that a chair is an inanimate object, and as such, it cannot desire companionship. His joke relies on the reader's knowledge of this fact.

Polysyndeton

- *The Door in the Wall*, "He hoped that <u>William or John</u>, <u>Thomas or Roger</u> would come in to tell him the news, but when their voices grew faint, he knew they had gone on past" (p. 8).

Robin's loneliness makes him long for someone—anyone—to visit him. The author could have simply listed all four names in a standard grammatical style: William, John, Thomas, or Roger. Adding the extra conjunction drags out the list and balances the four names, so that readers know that Thomas is equally as important as William and Roger is equally as important as John.

- *Number the Stars*, "'I think that is not true,' Uncle Henrik said. 'I think you are like your mama, <u>and</u> like your papa, <u>and</u> like me'" (p. 76).

Uncle Henrik adds a conjunction between each of the three items in the list. As a result, he makes all three comparisons equally important. Annemarie is not like all three people, collectively; she is like each one of them, separately.

- *The Lion, the Witch and the Wardrobe*, "Edmund felt much better as he began to sip the hot drink. It was something he had never tasted before, very sweet <u>and</u> foamy <u>and</u> creamy, and it warmed him right down to his toes" (p. 36).

Rather than experiencing the drink as sweet, foamy, and creamy all at once, Edmund experiences these sensations one at a time. The author's use of polysyndeton imitates the way we often taste something new or unfamiliar. We identify one feature at a time and compare it to other foods or drinks we have tasted in the past.

Rhyme

- *The Secret Garden*, "He sang it until the other children heard and laughed, too; and the crosser Mary got, the more they sang 'Mistress <u>Mary</u>, Quite <u>Contrary</u>'; and after that as long as she stayed with them they called her 'Mistress Mary Quite Contrary'" (p. 12).

This episode demonstrates one way that rhyme can be used to demonstrate humor or to create a mischievous tone. Rhyme can also be used in a serious manner, but this scene shows children playing with words and producing rhyme.

- *The Magician's Nephew*, "What it said was something like this—at least this is the sense of it though the poetry, when you read it there, was better.
   Make your choice, adventurous <u>Stranger</u>,
   Strike the bell and bide the <u>danger</u>,
   Or wonder, till it drives you <u>mad</u>,
   What would have followed if you <u>had</u>" (p. 54).

Rhyme is one indication that you have switched from prose to poetry, so it is sometimes used for formal or solemn situations. When Digory and Polly find the pillar in the Hall of Images, the writing on it is in poetry, giving them (and the reader) a sense of age and ceremony.

- *A Gathering of Days*, "How welcome is the pretty bird
    Who sits upon the tree;
    Nor would I ask for gold or ~~silver~~ silk
    As Spring is wealth for me" (p. 49).

From time to time, the fictional character Catherine adds to her journal snippets of poetry, bits of news, and jokes or adages popular in her time. This poem practices a simple form of rhyme. When you study a poem, one of the things you should look for is its "rhyme scheme," which means the pattern of rhyming and non-rhyming lines in the poem. The first line is always designated "A." If the second line rhymes with the first, it is also marked "A." If it does not rhyme, it becomes "B." If the third line rhymes with the first, it is marked "A." If it rhymes with the second, it becomes "B." If it does not rhyme with either, it becomes "C." The rhyme scheme for Catherine's poem, then, is ABCB.

Simile

- *The Door in the Wall*, "But his legs would not obey him. They were like two long pieces of uncooked dough, he thought, such as Jon-the-Cook rolled out on his molding board" (p. 10).

Illness caused Robin to lose the use of his legs and he attempts to describe that feeling. You can learn a great deal about a character by the type of similes he uses. This simile demonstrates that Robin is familiar with cooking and food preparation. As a writer, the similes used by your characters should reflect what is most familiar to them and what they would be likely to encounter in everyday life.

- *The Bronze Bow*, "All day long the giant was at the boy's heels, and at night he slept so close that Daniel could barely stretch his legs without kicking him. It was like being chained to a huge rock, having to drag it with him wherever he went" (p. 30).

Daniel feels responsible for Samson, and he compares the relationship to being shackled to a stone. Although he does not literally drag Samson behind him, he must remind Samson to do simple things like eating, almost as if the man were an inanimate object.

- *The Lion, the Witch and the Wardrobe*, "He was only a little taller than Lucy herself and he carried over his head an umbrella, white with snow. From the waist upwards he was like a man, but his legs were shaped like a goat's (the hair on them was glossy black) and instead of feet he had goat's hoofs" (pp. 9–10).

Simile is an important tool for writers of fantasy and science fiction because their readers do not have first-hand experience with fauns or satyrs or gnomes. Comparing a new or fantastical creature to familiar ones is one way to guide readers through the new encounter.

Synecdoche

- *Number the Stars*, "Annemarie stared up. There were two of them. That meant two helmets, two sets of cold eyes glaring at her, and four tall shiny boots planted firmly on the sidewalk, blocking her path to home" (p. 2).

When Annemarie and her friend Ellen meet two German soldiers on the streets of Copenhagen, she describes them based on a limited number of physical attributes. In her mind, a pair of eyes, a helmet, and a pair of boots is enough to identify a soldier.

- *Amos Fortune, Free Man*, "Amos grew from tall lean boyhood to strong and muscular manhood under the Copeland roof" (p. 43).

The reader understands from context and personal experience that Amos did not grow up under a bare roof; he grew up in a house. However, because the important detail is that Amos grows up under the Copelands' protection, and because the roof is a visible and regular feature of most houses, the Copelands' roof is able to stand in for their house as a whole.

- *A Gathering of Days*, "These be the thoughts of my heart: that I may remain here for ever and ever; here in this house which my father has built with the labour of his two hands" (p. 6).

Catherine's father built the house with his whole body, not just his hands, but the hands are understood to be closely associated with physical labor; the word "manual" comes from the Latin word *manus*, meaning "hand." In this case, "hands" are understood to stand in for work done personally and with physical effort.

For Further Reading

Greenholt, Jen. *Words Aptly Spoken: Children's Literature*. 2nd ed. West End, NC: Classical Conversations MultiMedia, 2010.

Harmon, William, and Hugh Holman. *A Handbook to Literature*. 10th ed. Upper Saddle River, NJ: Pearson/Prentice Hall, 2006.

Kern, Andrew. *The Lost Tools of Writing: Level 1*. 4th ed. Concord, NC: The CiRCE Institute, 2011.

Bibliography

Angeli, Marguerite de. *The Door in the Wall*. New York: Bantam Doubleday Dell Books for Young Readers, 1990. Print.

Avi. *Crispin: The Cross of Lead*. New York: Hyperion Books, 2004. Print.

Blos, Joan W. *A Gathering of Days: A New England Girl's Journal, 1830–32*. 2nd ed. New York: Aladdin Books, 1990. Print.

Burnett, Frances Hodgson. *The Secret Garden*. New York: Aladdin Classics, 1999. Print.

Latham, Jean Lee. *Carry On, Mr. Bowditch*. Illustr. John O'Hara Cosgrave, II. Boston: Houghton Mifflin, 1983. Print.

Lewis, C. S. *The Lion, the Witch and the Wardrobe* [1950]. *The Chronicles of Narnia*. Illustr. Pauline Baynes. New York: HarperTrophy, 1998. Print.

---. *The Magician's Nephew* [1955]. *The Chronicles of Narnia*. Illustr. Pauline Baynes. New York: HarperTrophy, 1998. Print.

Lowry, Lois. *Number the Stars*. Boston: Houghton Mifflin, 1989. Print.

Speare, Elizabeth George. *The Bronze Bow*. Boston: Houghton Mifflin, 1989. Print.

Yates, Elizabeth. *Amos Fortune, Free Man*. Illustr. Nora S. Unwin. New York: Puffin Books, 1989. Print.

EXAMPLES FROM

Challenge B

LITERATURE

Examples from Challenge B Literature

You will encounter many different writing styles in Challenge B and will also have the opportunity to practice your own creative writing. As you prepare to put these rhetorical tools to work for you, you can gain a great deal by studying the way other authors have used them. Pay close attention to the kinds of literary techniques used in different genres of literature, and begin to think about which rhetorical devices best suit your own writing style. These examples are taken from classic children's literature.

Alliteration

- *Where the Red Fern Grows*, "We stood and listened to the beautiful music, the deep-throated notes of <u>h</u>unting <u>h</u>ounds on the <u>h</u>ot-scented trail of a river coon" (p. 130).

Even though Wilson Rawls had little formal education and may not have named these rhetorical devices in his writing, his effort to describe the beautiful music of the hounds uses both alliteration (repetition of the consonant "h") and assonance (repetition of vowel sounds in "throated notes"). First, the sound of the letter "h" suggests the sound of a dog panting or a human breathing heavily. Second, have you ever heard a dog howl? The noise is almost entirely composed of long vowel sounds. In this case, alliteration and assonance enable Rawls to imitate the howling of the hounds and capture the sound of the scene in the words he uses to describe it.

Allusion

- *Little Britches*, "Mother used to recite 'The Charge of the Light Brigade.' <u>With all the guns and running horses</u>, I was sure I was in it" (p. 28).

"The Charge of the Light Brigade" is a poem by British poet Alfred Lord Tennyson. The poem, which is set in 1854 during the Crimean War in Russia, begins, "Half a league, half a league, / Half a league onward, / All in the valley of Death / Rode the six hundred." The poem describes an actual event, in which miscommunication led a sabre-armed cavalry unit to charge a well-armed Russian artillery unit and be decimated by cannon fire. The poem was often cited as an example of valor under daunting circumstances, and Ralph may be using it in this way.

- *The Hiding Place*, "Mama threw her arms around her and they clung together. But I stood rooted to the spot, knowing <u>that I had seen a mystery. It was Father's train ticket</u>, given at the moment itself" (p. 40).

Corrie makes an internal allusion as she observes the faith of her dying aunt. Earlier in the book, she had related a story in which her father explained that God gives each individual the strength to face death at the right moment: "'Corrie,' he began gently, 'when you and I go to Amsterdam—when do I give you your ticket?'

I sniffed a few times, considering this.

'Why, just before we get on the train.'

'Exactly. And our wise Father in heaven knows when we're going to need things, too. Don't run out ahead of Him, Corrie. When the time comes that some of us will have to die, you will look into your heart and find the strength you need—just in time'" (p. 29).

Anaphora

- *The Hiding Place*, "A truck was parked in front of the fish mart; into the back were climbing men, women, and children, all wearing the yellow star. There was no reason we could see why this particular place at this particular time had been chosen.

'Father! <u>Those poor people!</u>' I cried.

The police line opened, the truck moved through. We watched till it turned the corner.

'Those poor people,' Father echoed. But to my surprise I saw that he was looking at the soldiers now forming into ranks to march away. 'I pity the poor Germans, Corrie. They have touched the apple of God's eye'" (pp. 68–69).

Because Father's statement does not follow immediately after Corrie's, this is an imperfect instance of anaphora, which typically refers to successive clauses or sentences. However, it demonstrates the fact that anaphora can be used to show contrast as well as emphasis. In this passage, both Corrie and her father respond to the arrest of Dutch Jews with the same opening exclamation; however, while Corrie directs her sentiment toward the deported Jews, Father feels pity for the Germans arresting them.

Antithesis

❂ *The Hiding Place*, "The squat little man stared from one of us to the other. Slowly the heavy-rimmed eyes filled with tears. 'Are they well?' he repeated. 'I believe they are well. I hope that they are well. They are dead'" (p. 72).

To most readers, being well and being dead are contradictory states of being. One cannot be well if one is dead. When Mr. de Vries claims that his dogs are well and also dead, an example of antithesis, he calls attention to how unnatural life in Holland has become. He has put his dogs to sleep deliberately, preferring to give them a merciful death than to abandon them to an uncertain fate should he and his family be taken away by the Germans.

Apostrophe

❂ *The Hiding Place*, "Adventure and anguish, horror and heaven were just around the corner, and we did not know. Oh Father! Betsie! If I had known would I have gone ahead? Could I have done the things I did?" (p. 7).

In the first chapter of *The Hiding Place*, Corrie relates the events of an earlier day, before the events of the Holocaust. The passage above breaks away from the narrative time (1937) as Corrie reveals that she is looking back from the time of writing (1971), a time when neither Father nor Betsie is alive. Although they are absent, she calls their names as if they were present. In addition to demonstrating apostrophe, this passage is a good example of foreshadowing, when an author gives the reader clues about what is to come. In this case, the author foreshadows the deaths of Father and Betsie.

Assonance

❂ *The Phantom Tollbooth*, "Mile after

mile after

mile after

mile he dr<u>o</u>ve, and now, gradually, the car went sl<u>o</u>wer and sl<u>o</u>wer, until it was hardly moving at all.

'It looks as though I'm getting n<u>o</u>where,' yawned Mil<u>o</u>, becoming very drowsy and dull" (p. 22).

The Phantom Tollbooth is an excellent example of a book that uses form to reinforce its content. Notice the use of anaphora: the author starts each repeated phrase "mile after" on a new line, as if it were poetry. The reader has to work hard but does not get any further into the sentence, just as Milo's journey slows down in the Doldrums. The vowel sounds contribute to this effect as well. The repetition of the long "o" sound mimics the sound of someone yawning. Instead of simply saying, "Milo yawned," the author uses assonance to imitate the sound of a yawn.

Asyndeton

❂ *Where the Red Fern Grows*, "There in the window was the most wonderful sight I had ever seen; everything under the sun; overalls, jackets, bolts of beautiful cloth, new harnesses, collars, bridles; and then my eyes did pop open" (p. 29).

To Billy's inexperienced eyes, the town store overflows with an unimaginable variety of goods. His list of items demonstrates asyndeton (grammar would call for an "and" between "collars" and "bridles"), and the overall structure of the list (independent clauses joined by semicolons) piles up items in such a way that the reader feels almost as overwhelmed as Billy does.

❂ *The Hiding Place*, "The other shops up and down the narrow street were shuttered and silent: the optician's next door, the dress shop, the baker's, Weil's Furriers across the street" (p. 3).

As Corrie describes the early morning hours in Haarlem, she makes a statement about the other shops on the street and then follows it with a list of examples. The list lacks a final coordinating conjunction, and in this case, her use of asyndeton gives the impression that her list is incomplete. There may be other shops in the row, but she has given only a few examples for the sake of space.

Chiasmus

- *The Phantom Tollbooth*, "When he was in school, he longed to be out, and when he was out he longed to be in. On the way he thought about coming home, and coming home he thought about going" (p. 9).

This passage has two examples of chiasmus. The first is "when in, longed out"; "when out, longed in." The prepositions "out" and "in" are inverted in the second half of the sentence, but nothing else changes. Likewise, in the second example, the adverbial phrases "on the way/going" and "coming home" switch places. Milo is so dissatisfied with the world that he dislikes not only one activity but also its opposite, the thing he professed to desire. In this way, the form of writing—not merely the content—expresses the proverb, "The grass is always greener on the other side of the fence."

Consonance

- *The Phantom Tollbooth*, "He drew from his cape a small heavy box about the size of a schoolbook and handed it ceremoniously to Milo.

'In this box are all the words I know,' he said. Most of them you will never need, some you will use constantly, but with them you may ask all the questions which have never been answered and answer all the questions which have never been asked. All the great books of the past and all the ones yet to come are made with these words" (pp. 98–99).

King Azaz does not rhyme (Rhyme and Reason are absent from his kingdom), but he does demonstrate consonance. For example, the words "box" and "books" have the same initial and concluding consonants, but different vowel sounds. Consonance is a form of imperfect rhyme.

Epistrophe

- *The Phantom Tollbooth*, "The Mathemagician stopped what he was doing and explained simply, 'Why, in a box that's so small you can't see it—and that's kept in a drawer that's so small that you can't see it, in a dresser that's so small you can't see it, in a house that's so small you can't see it, on a street that's so small you can't see it, in a city that's so small you can't see it, which is part of a country that's so small you can't see it, in a world that's so small you can't see it'" (p. 191).

The Mathemagician has been trying to explain to Milo the concept of the smallest number and the number of the greatest possible magnitude. Attempting to reach those numbers is an impossible endeavor. Using the device of epistrophe, the Mathemagician shows Milo in this passage how impossible it would be.

Foreshadowing

- "The Hammer of God," "He seemed to live for nothing but his religion; but there were some who said…that it was a love of Gothic architecture rather than of God…Indeed the charge was mostly an ignorant misunderstanding of the love of solitude and secret prayer, and was founded on his being often found kneeling, not before the altar, but in peculiar places, in the crypts or gallery, or even in the belfry" (*Words Aptly Spoken: Short Stories*, p. 194).

When you first read this line about Rev. Wilfred Bohun's love of high places in the church, it might seem meaningless. Only when you have finished reading the story and returned to it a second time would you notice that Chesterton has laid out this bit of detail as a clue to the end of the story.

- "The Bet," "The banker, who was younger and more nervous in those days, was suddenly carried away by excitement" (*Words Aptly Spoken: Short Stories*, p. 28).

As Chekhov sets the scene for his story, he uses several instances of foreshadowing. In this line, he gives the reader a clue that something has happened to make the banker's temperament change. The reader does not know yet what has happened, but this foreshadowing makes us curious to learn more.

Hyperbole

- *Where the Red Fern Grows*, "I reached way back in Arkansas somewhere. By the time my fist had traveled all the way down to the Cherokee Strip, there was a lot of power behind it. Smack on the end of Freck's nose it exploded" (p. 40).

As Billy begins to hit the town boy, he is not literally reaching his fist across state lines (no one's arm is that long!), but this exaggeration shows how much energy and preparation Billy put into his punch.

- *Little Britches*, "When I was tightening up my cinches after dinner, Hi came over and noticed that the end of one of my fingers was bleeding. He slapped me on the back so hard it made my teeth rattle, and said, 'You stop frettin' 'bout that old cayuse or you'll have your fingers et clear down to the knuckles'" (p. 217).

Ralph has been biting his fingernails because he is afraid for his horse's safety. ("Cayuse" is a word cowboys used to refer to a wild or common horse.) His friend Hi knows that he will not literally chew off his fingers, but Hi exaggerates to make a point to Ralph.

Imagery

- *The Hiding Place*, "It was a chill raw morning in late May: after three months in prison I had been called for my first hearing. […] And then I saw something. Whoever used the fourth of the huts had planted a row of tulips along the side. They were wilted now, only tall stems and yellowing leaves, but…'Dear Lord, let me go to hut number four!'" (p. 158).

In this passage, made vivid by the description of wilted yellow tulips, Corrie shares with the reader something she was able to discern about the officer who used that hut. Because he had taken care to provide a spot of color in the gray environment, she hoped (rightly) that he might have a spot of compassion in his nature.

- "The Celestial Railroad," "Our coach rattled out of the city, and at a short distance from its outskirts passed over a bridge of elegant construction, but somewhat too slight, as I imagined, to sustain any considerable weight. On both sides lay an extensive quagmire, which could not have been more disagreeable either to sight or smell had all the kennels of the earth emptied their pollution there" (*Words Aptly Spoken: Short Stories*, p. 145).

Hawthorne uses imagery masterfully, not only in novels, such as *The Scarlet Letter*, but also in his short stories. When he describes the bridge, he is describing a physical bridge, but he is also using it to make a point. Readers are later told that the bridge over the Slough of Despond is made of philosophy and scientific rationalism. These building materials may be elegant, but they are not solid as a means of keeping pilgrims out of despair.

In the second example, readers may not know what the "Slough of Despond" in John Bunyan's famous allegory *The Pilgrim's Progress* was supposed to smell like, but in Hawthorne's retelling of that famous story, he invites readers to imagine the smell as the waste from many doghouses, a vivid description that expresses the feeling of being mired in despair.

Litotes

- *The Phantom Tollbooth*, "'As you can see, that leaves almost no time for brooding, lagging, plodding, or procrastinating, and if we stopped to think or laugh, we'd never get nothing done.'

'You mean you'd never get anything done,' corrected Milo.

'We don't want to get anything done,' snapped another angrily; 'we want to get nothing done, and we can do that without your help'" (p. 27).

Some authors use rhetorical devices to generate humorous wordplay, and *The Phantom Tollbooth* is a perfect example. In this scene, the Lethargarian seems to use a double negative, and Milo rebukes him for his poor grammar. However, according to the rules of the fictional country called the Doldrums, the primary responsibility of the inhabitants is to do nothing, so the Lethargarian is actually using litotes to say, "If we stopped to think or laugh, we'd get something done."

- *The Hiding Place*, "But during the first months of occupation, life was not so very unbearable" (p. 64).

If Corrie were to use direct statement in this instance, she would say that life was bearable. This more complicated structure allows her to contrast expectations and reality: she dreaded occupation, thinking that it would immediately produce hardship and suffering, and she was surprised to find that it did not. On the other hand, litotes also contribute to narrative foreshadowing. When Corrie says that life was not unbearable during the first few months, the unspoken remainder of her statement is that life became unbearable not long afterward.

Metaphor

- *The Hiding Place*, "A full ten years ago, way back in 1927, Willem had written in his doctoral thesis, done in Germany, that a terrible evil was taking root in that land. Right at the university, he said, seeds were being planted of a contempt for human life such as the world had never seen" (p. 13).

Corrie ten Boom's brother Willem uses an agricultural metaphor to describe the evil developing in Germany. Evil does not "take root" or "plant seeds" in literal soil, but, like a weed, it can grow in secret long before it becomes visible. Keep in mind that the same kind of metaphor can be used for positive phenomena, such as hope or faith (see Matthew 17:20).

- "The Notorious Jumping Frog of Calaveras County," "Simon Wheeler backed me into a corner and blockaded me there with his chair, and then sat down and reeled off the monotonous narrative which follows this paragraph. He never smiled, he never frowned, he never changed his voice from the gentle-flowing key to which he tuned his initial sentence, he never betrayed the slightest suspicion of enthusiasm; but all through the interminable narrative there ran a vein of impressive earnestness and sincerity..." (*Words Aptly Spoken: Short Stories*, p. 215).

Twain begins his short story with several metaphors that give the sense of old Simon Wheeler, the storyteller. His voice is described as a guitar or other stringed instrument that is tuned to a certain key and does not vary from it. Next, his story is described as though it were a dense rock with a thin vein of gold running through the center. Combined, these music and mining metaphors help Twain establish the folksy, rough-edged nature of his character.

Metonymy

- *Where the Red Fern Grows*, "Looking in the buggy I saw my ax. I didn't think I ever wanted to see it again, but for some reason it didn't look like I thought it would. There was no blood on it and it looked harmless enough laying there all clean and bright" (p. 166).

In this scene, after a deadly hunting accident results in the death of a young boy, Billy sees his hunting ax again for the first time. Even though the ax itself is simply a tool for chopping down trees, Billy associates it with the accident. He feels the same anxiety and revulsion that he felt when the accident first took place. He is surprised that it is not physically different because it has become so symbolic in his mind. This is an instance of metonymy, when a concrete object stands in for a larger or more abstract concept with which it is associated.

Onomatopoeia

- *Where the Red Fern Grows*, "Up out of that snarling, growling, slashing mass reared an old redbone hound" (p. 2).

When you say the words "snarl" or "growl," the pronunciation is almost identical to the sounds the words represent. Reading this sentence aloud, you can almost hear the sound of the fighting dogs reproduced in the words used to describe it.

Parallelism

- *Where the Red Fern Grows*, "'Remember, Billy said a prayer when he asked for his pups and then there were your prayers. Billy got his pups. Through those dogs, your prayers were answered. Yes, I'm sure it is a miracle'" (p. 240).

Papa's explanation is an example of parallelism in terms of content. He lists two parallel prayers: 1a) Billy's prayer, and 2a) Mama's prayer. He then shows how each prayer received a parallel answer: 1b) Billy got his puppies, and 2b) Mama got her wish that the family would be able to move into town.

Personification

- *Little Britches*, "Muriel's cat thought she ought to give some presents, too, and she must have counted noses, because she had a litter of five kittens Christmas Eve" (p. 184).

Although a cat probably does not count noses, does not know it is Christmas, and cannot change the number of kittens she is carrying to suit her design, Ralph describes her as though she were capable of acting in this way. He ascribes human motives to her in order to express something that could not be explained according to logic, or would lose its charm if it were.

Polysyndeton

- *The Phantom Tollbooth,* "'As you can see, though, I'm <u>neither</u> tall <u>nor</u> short <u>nor</u> fat <u>nor</u> thin. In fact, I'm quite ordinary, but there are so many ordinary men that no one asks their opinion about anything'" (p. 14).

Polysyndeton gives equal weight to each of the adjectives in this sentence. Milo's host is pretending to be four different people at the same time, each completely separate and distinct from the others, so the sentence structure is particularly appropriate to the content of the scene.

Rhyme

- *The Hiding Place,* "'Can you recite the One Hundred and Sixty-sixth Psalm, Opa?' Meyer said. Father beamed. Of course there is no Psalm 166; the Psalter stops with 150. It must be a joke, and nothing could please Father better than a scriptural joke" (p. 101).

This example of rhyme is slightly different than others you have studied. Writers may not consciously use rhyme when writing prose, but they can use references to poetry like this one to add depth to the setting and tell you about the culture of a family or a nation. Father's ability to recognize a joke about the Psalms tells you how familiar he was with Scripture. When you read, pay attention to the poetry the characters read and recite. You will learn a great deal about their world.

- *Little Britches,* "He pointed his finger right at me and said, 'You! Little tow-headed fella! Go to the board and write me: <u>"Pare a pear with a pair of scissors."</u> The only two kinds I knew about were pear and pair, and I got all mixed up on whether there were two s's or two z's in scissors" (pp. 126–127).

In this example, rhyme permits the author to create a pun. In spoken English, homophones (words pronounced the same but spelled differently or with different meanings) are difficult to represent. In writing, however, the reader can follow along and sense Ralph's frustration as he tries to learn the subtleties of the English language.

Simile

- *Where the Red Fern Grows,* "One was large with long, upright handles that stood out <u>like wings on a morning dove</u>. The highly polished surface gleamed and glistened with a golden sheen. The other was smaller and made of silver. It was neat and trim, and sparkled <u>like a white star in the heavens</u>" (p. 6).

To describe the two trophies, the adult Billy uses familiar, concrete sights (wings on a morning [*sic*] dove and a white star in the heavens) to give readers a point of reference for the way he sees the handles of a trophy and the gleam of the silver cup.

- *Little Britches,* "Away toward the south there were brown, rolling hills, <u>as though the tablecloth had been wrinkled a little</u>. And not far beyond it, toward the west, the hogbacks rose <u>like big loaves of golden-brown bread</u> sitting on the table" (p. 12).

Seeking to describe the land surrounding his family's new ranch, Ralph turns to domestic similes. He has seen bread rising and tablecloths wrinkling in his New Hampshire home, but the countryside outside of Denver is something entirely new. The only things to which he can compare it are things he already knows. For this reason, he uses a known setting (his home) to make sense of the unknown (the range).

Synecdoche

- *Where the Red Fern Grows,* "Arriving home, I dumped the sack of candy out on the bed. <u>Six little hands helped themselves</u>. I was well repaid by the love and adoration I saw in the wide blue eyes of my three little sisters" (p. 24).

The reader knows that Billy's sisters, not their disembodied hands, are reaching into the pile of candy. In this instance of synecdoche, the hands (the most important body part for grabbing) stand in for the girls themselves.

For Further Reading

Greenholt, Jen. *Words Aptly Spoken: Children's Literature.* 2nd ed. West End, NC: Classical Conversations MultiMedia, 2010.

Harmon, William, and Hugh Holman. *A Handbook to Literature.* 10th ed. Upper Saddle River, NJ: Pearson/Prentice Hall, 2006.

Kern, Andrew. *The Lost Tools of Writing: Level 1.* 4th ed. Concord, NC: The CiRCE Institute, 2011.

Bibliography

Boom, Corrie ten, John Sherrill, and Elizabeth Sherrill. *The Hiding Place*. New York: Bantam, 1974. Print.

Chekov, Anton. "The Bet." *Words Aptly Spoken: Short Stories*. 3rd ed. Ed. Jen Greenholt. West End, NC: Classical Conversations MultiMedia, 2014. Print.

Chesterton, G. K. "The Hammer of God." *Words Aptly Spoken: Short Stories*. 3rd ed. Ed. Jen Greenholt. West End, NC: Classical Conversations MultiMedia, 2014. Print.

Hawthorne, Nathaniel. "The Celestial Railroad." *Words Aptly Spoken: Short Stories*. 3rd ed. Ed. Jen Greenholt. West End, NC: Classical Conversations MultiMedia, 2014. Print.

Juster, Norton. *The Phantom Tollbooth*. 35th Anniversary Edition. Illustr. Jules Feiffer. New York: Random House, 1996. Print.

Moody, Ralph. *Little Britches: Father and I Were Ranchers*. Illustr. Edward Shenton. Lincoln, NE: Bison Books, 1991. Print.

Rawls, Wilson. *Where the Red Fern Grows*. New York: Dell Laurel-Leaf, 2001. Print.

Twain, Mark. "The Notorious Jumping Frog of Calaveras County." *Words Aptly Spoken: Short Stories*. 3rd ed. Ed. Jen Greenholt. West End, NC: Classical Conversations MultiMedia, 2014. Print.

EXAMPLES FROM

Challenge I

LITERATURE

Examples from Challenge I Literature

From the sermons of Cotton Mather to the poetry of Henry Wadsworth Longfellow and the novels of Mark Twain, American literature encompasses a broad range of genres, styles, and subjects. Although American authors have borrowed from a legacy of British and other world literatures, they have also created new, unique forms influenced by the diverse landscape, history, and cultures that make up the United States. These examples are taken from a selection of classic American novels, stories, essays, and poems. Some authors use rhetorical devices deliberately to add flair, while others write in a simple style modeled on the speech of average Americans, demonstrating that even everyday speech can be beautiful. Learning to recognize the rhetorical devices we use unawares will give you a new appreciation for the richness of the English language.

All of these classic books are available in multiple editions, so unless you are using the same edition as the one cited in the bibliography, page numbers may not match precisely.

Alliteration

- *An Old-Fashioned Girl*, "I was wakeful and lay listening to the crickets till the clock struck twelve; then I got drowsy, and was just dropping of[f] when the sound of steps outside woke me up staring wide awake" (p. 99).

Grandma's narrative demonstrates how our speech sometimes changes when we begin to tell stories. This passage creates suspense using multiple examples of alliteration on the consonants "w," "s," "d," "l," and "c." The letters "w" and "s," in particular, create a whispering sound. As a whole, alliteration adds poetic flair, but it also encourages us to pay attention to the speaker's words.

- "The Ransom of Red Chief," "There was a sylvan attitude of somnolent sleepiness pervading that section of the external outward surface of Alabama that lay exposed to my view" (*Words Aptly Spoken: American Literature*, p. 35).

The incongruity between Sam's occupation and his manner of speaking is a source of humor in this story. He is a kidnapper and con man, but he has an enormous vocabulary, and he speaks in elaborate sentences with archaic phrasing and formal style. His use of alliteration to describe the sleepy village not only makes this story enjoyable to read aloud, it also provides character development.

Allusion

- *To Kill a Mockingbird*, "Mindful of John Wesley's strictures on the use of many words in buying and selling, Simon made a pile practicing medicine, but in this pursuit he was unhappy lest he be tempted into doing what he knew was not for the glory of God, as the putting on of gold and costly apparel" (p. 4).

Sometimes research is necessary to identify an unfamiliar allusion. John Wesley (1703–1791), one of the founders of the Methodist church, wrote extensively about the character of a Christian and the standards of the church. His *General Rules of the Methodist Church* (1808 edition) exhorts believers against harmful behaviors, such as "Fighting, quarreling, brawling, brother going to law with brother; returning evil for evil, or railing for railing; the using many words in buying or selling" and "The putting on of gold and costly apparel"[1]

---

[1] From *The Book of Discipline of The United Methodist Church* (The United Methodist Publishing House, 2004). Accessed from the archives of the United Methodist Church, http://archives.umc.org.

- *An Old-Fashioned Girl*, "'Fire away, Polly,' said the young <u>sultan</u>, one evening, as his little <u>Scheherazade</u> sat down in her low chair, after stirring up the fire till the room was bright and cozy" (p. 60).

When you first read this scene, you might not know that Scheherazade is the leading lady in *One Thousand and One Nights*, a collection of Arabic, Persian, Indian, and Egyptian folktales compiled during the Islamic Golden Age and translated into English in the eighteenth century. The collection is organized within a **frame story**, similar to the one in Chaucer's *The Canterbury Tales*. Scheherazade is brought before the sultan, who has a history of killing his brides after one night. To save her life, she begins to tell him stories. As long as she prolongs her story, he delays her death. The rest of the collection is comprised of the stories that she tells. Familiar figures such as Aladdin, Ali Baba, and Sinbad the Sailor are all characters in her stories. In *An Old-Fashioned Girl*, the author is comparing Tom to the spoiled king and Polly to his long-suffering but clever companion.

Anaphora

- *Essays to Do Good*, "<u>Much is requisite to be done</u> that the great God and his Christ may be more known and served in the world; and that the errors which prevent men from glorifying their Creator and Redeemer may be rectified. <u>Much is necessary to be done</u> that the evil manners of the world, by which men are drowned in perdition, may be reformed; and mankind rescued from the epidemical corruption which has overwhelmed it. <u>Much must be done</u> that the miseries of the world may have suitable remedies provided for them; and that the wretched may be relieved and comforted" (*Words Aptly Spoken: American Literature*, p. 57).

Anaphora does not always repeat word-for-word the opening phrase in subsequent clauses or sentences. It can be more effective rhetorically to vary your word choice slightly, as in this example. The repetition is identifiable but not exact, allowing the author to keep his audience's attention without seeming to repeat himself.

- "The Song of Hiawatha," "Should you ask me,
  <u>Whence</u> these stories?
  <u>Whence</u> these legends and traditions,
  <u>With</u> the odors of the forest
  <u>With</u> the dew and damp of meadows" (*Words Aptly Spoken: American Literature*, p. 79).

Rather than relying on rhyme, this poem is characterized by repetition of initial words and phrases, particularly in the introduction, as this example shows. Thanks to this device, the poem flows off the tongue smoothly, and each line paints a picture for the listener to imagine.

- *Up from Slavery*, "To those of the white race who look to the incoming of those of foreign birth and strange tongue and habits for the prosperity of the South, were I permitted I would repeat what I say to my own race, '<u>Cast down your bucket</u> where you are.' <u>Cast it down</u> among the eight millions of Negroes whose habits you know, whose fidelity and love you have tested in days when to have proved treacherous meant the ruin of your firesides. <u>Cast down your bucket</u> among these people who have, without strikes and labour wars, tilled your fields, cleared your forests, built your railroads and cities, and brought forth treasures from the bowels of the earth, and helped make possible this magnificent representation of the progress of the South" (p. 107).

Booker T. Washington's Atlanta Exposition address, reprinted in this book, is a masterpiece of rhetoric. One of the primary devices Washington employs is repetition, here used at the beginning of subsequent sentences or ideas. He creates a metaphor for the audience and then repeatedly refers back to it, reminding his listeners of his central argument. If they remember nothing else from his speech, he attempts to ensure that they will remember this message.

Antithesis

- *To Kill a Mockingbird*, "Then he took off his glasses and wiped them, and we saw another 'first': we had never seen him sweat—<u>he was one of those men whose faces never perspired, but now it was shining tan</u>" (p. 273).

Scout's surprise at her father's state is enhanced by the author's use of antithesis. Scout confronts a seeming contradiction: Atticus never sweats, yet Atticus is sweating now. For both Scout and the reader, this contradiction makes what is happening in the courtroom all the more momentous: it is powerful enough to reverse one of her father's defining characteristics.

- *Narrative of the Life of Frederick Douglass*, "He would <u>whip her to make her scream</u>, and <u>whip her to make her hush</u>" (p. 4).

Showing that the master whipped his slaves for one reason and also for the opposite reason is one technique by which the author demonstrates the unnatural cruelty of slavery. He also uses this device to disprove the argument that slaves had only to do their masters' bidding in order to avoid punishment.

Apostrophe

- *The Sign of the Beaver*, "So often, as he did the squaw work that Attean would have despised, thoughts of his mother filled his head. He imagined her moving about the cabin, humming her little tunes as she beat up a batch of corn bread, shaking out the boardcloth at the door—for of course she would not let them eat at a bare table. [...] <u>Sometimes he could almost hear the sound of her voice, and when he shut his eyes he could see her special smile.</u>

  He tried to think of ways to please her. She would need new dishes for the good meals she would cook" (pp. 124–125).

  Matt's story is not told in poetic form, but in this passage, he invokes his mother, who is absent, and talks about her as though she were present. She inspires his actions and directs his thoughts. The idea of his family and their needs and values drives Matt to continue improving the small cabin in their absence.

- *The Old Man and the Sea*, "I wish it were a dream and that I had never hooked him. <u>I'm sorry about it, fish</u>. It makes everything wrong" (p. 110).

  Having killed the great fish, the old man continues to speak to him as though he were alive. Alone on the boat, he talks to himself as well, but when he talks to the fish, his tone changes. He offers an apology because he recognizes in the fish's will to fight some of the bravery and determination he values so highly.

Assonance

- "The Song of Hiawatha," "I should answer, I should tell you

  'In the bird's-nests of the forest,

  In the lodges of the b<u>ea</u>ver,
  In the hoofprint of the bison
  In the eyry of the <u>ea</u>gle!'" (*Words Aptly Spoken: American Literature*, p. 80).

  Although "The Song of Hiawatha" does not rely on precise rhyme, it does contain some examples of near rhyme, including assonance. In this example, the words "beaver" and "eagle" do not have the same final consonant, but the vowel sound in the final stressed syllable does match. When you say the word "beaver," you put more emphasis on the first syllable, "bea." Likewise, when you say the word "eagle," you emphasize the first syllable, "ea."

Asyndeton

- *Through Gates of Splendor*, "Were it not that I believed that Jesus was seen of men and proved Himself to be supernatural in outwitting death, I would throw the whole system back to the troubled skies and take a raft down the Mississippi today. But <u>the fact is founding, settling, establishing</u>" (p. 8).

  Jim's use of asyndeton in his journal prevents the list of attributes from becoming a hierarchy, with the first weighted more heavily than the last. Nor do founding, settling, and establishing occur in sequence for him; they are, together, a proven fact in his life.

- *The Call of the Wild*, "Their irritability arose out of their misery, <u>increased with it</u>, <u>doubled upon it</u>, <u>out-distanced it</u>" (p. 37).

  Some writers use asyndeton to set the mood of a story. Just as a character who speaks in short, simple sentences makes a different impression on readers than one who speaks in long-winded, eloquent prose, so too a novel written in short, terse sentences lacking conjunctions has a different tone than one written in long, rambling sentences. In this example, the harsh conditions of the Arctic may be better expressed in language that has been stripped of excess words and precise grammar.

Chiasmus

- *Narrative of the Life of Frederick Douglass*, "Mr. Gore was a grave man, and, though a young man, he indulged in no jokes, said no funny words, seldom smiled. <u>His words were in perfect keeping with his looks, and <u>his looks were in perfect keeping with his words</u>" (p. 13).

As described, Mr. Gore is a consistent man as well as a cruel one. Douglass frequently points out that the horrendous behavior of slave owners and overseers is not an exception; it is the natural conclusion of the institution in the South. This rhetorical device makes a similar point.

- "A Model of Christian Charity," "In all these and like cases Christ was a general rule. (Matt. 7:22), 'Whatsoever ye would that <u>men should do to you, do ye the same to them also</u>'" (*Words Aptly Spoken: American Literature*, p. 54).

The Golden Rule is a prime example of chiasmus. The second half of the clause inverts the subject and the object of the preposition from the first half: men should do [whatsoever] to you; you do the same to them. This precept teaches balance not just in its meaning but also in its grammatical structure.

Consonance

- "The Ransom of Red Chief," "'You won't take me back home again, Snake-eye, will you?'

'Not right away,' says I. '<u>We'll</u> stay here in the cave a <u>while</u>.'

'All right!' says he. 'That'll be <u>fine</u>. I never had such <u>fun</u> in all my life'" (*Words Aptly Spoken: American Literature*, p. 35).

In this example, the two pairs of underlined words begin and end with the same consonants ("w" and "l" in the first set, "f" and "n" in the second set) but have different vowel sounds, demonstrating consonance. Master storytellers know that the sound of a story can capture the listeners' ears, soothe their moods, or excite their curiosity. Devices, such as consonance, may or may not be used deliberately, but they show the versatility of the English language in appealing to multiple senses.

- "The Pit and the Pendulum," "I saw that the decrees of what to me was Fate, were still issuing from those lips. I saw them writhe with a deadly locution. I saw them fashion the syllables of my name; and I <u>shuddered</u> because no <u>sound</u> <u>succeeded</u>" (p. 63).

Poe is an exemplary writer of dark and threatening stories. He uses grammatical structure, sound, and imagery to create this effect. In this example, the three underlined words begin and end with the same consonant sounds: "s" and "d," respectively. The repetition of the letter "s" creates a hissing sound that matches the context of the surrounding sentences. Look back at the preceding line. The narrator describes his judges' words as "writhing" in a deadly manner, as if they were poisonous snakes. The final "d" sound, particularly in "succeeded," repeats the sound of the word "deadly," further adding to the ominous quality of this opening scene.

Epistrophe

- "The Method of Grace," "And, therefore, people from time to time must be taught how far they must go, and what must be wrought in them, <u>before they can speak peace to their hearts</u>. This is what I design at present, that I may deliver my soul, that I may be free from the blood of those to whom I preach—that I may not fail to declare the whole counsel of God. I shall, from the words of the text, endeavor to show you what you must undergo, and what must be wrought in you <u>before you can speak peace to your hearts</u>" (*Words Aptly Spoken: American Literature*, p. 62).

Many early American preachers were master rhetoricians. Some, but not all, were great orators, so they relied on rhetorical tools to make their sermons memorable to the large crowds to whom they spoke. Repetition is one of the most important tools of memory, as in this example of epistrophe. The author reiterates his central message at the end of subsequent points to emphasize what he wants his audience to remember.

- "The Song of Hiawatha," "Ever rising, rising, rising
Till it touched the top of <u>heaven</u>,
Till it broke against the <u>heaven</u>,
And rolled outward all around it" (*Words Aptly Spoken: American Literature*, p. 83).

This passage demonstrates both anaphora and epistrophe, repeating both the first and last words in two subsequent lines. Because the opening and closing elements of the lines are the same, the reader's attention is drawn to the center of each line: the verbs "touched" and "broke." As a writer, you can use a similar device to focus your reader's attention on something specific. Think about a mystery scene:

you might place characters in a room that is familiar to them, but change one small detail. The observant reader's gaze will be drawn to that unfamiliar item without your having to tell them it is there.

Foreshadowing

- *The Scarlet Letter*, "By the Indian's side, and evidently sustaining a companionship with him, stood a white man, <u>clad in a strange disarray of civilized and savage costume</u>" (p. 82).

Authors often use description to foreshadow something about a character's role in the story. A character's name may do the same thing—most explicitly in allegories such as *The Pilgrim's Progress*. When Hawthorne first introduces the character Roger Chillingworth, he uses this phrase, "clad in a strange disarray of civilized and savage costume" to reveal something about Chillingworth's nature.

Hyperbole

- *Up from Slavery*, "The picture of several dozen boys and girls in a schoolroom engaged in study made a deep impression upon me, and I had the feeling that <u>to get into a schoolhouse and study in this way would be about the same as getting into paradise</u>" (p. 4).

Washington is not really equating going to school with enjoying eternal bliss; however, to make his point, he uses selective exaggeration to show readers how much he desired to learn and how much he regretted being barred from the schoolhouse on the basis of his race.

- *The Call of the Wild*, "For the last time in his life he allowed passion to usurp cunning and reason, and it was because of his great love for John Thornton that <u>he lost his head</u>" (p. 60).

To "lose your head" in anger or passion is a familiar expression. In fact, it is so familiar that we sometimes forget that it is an example of figurative language. In this scene, we know that Buck does not misplace his skull, nor is it chopped off. We take the author's exaggeration as a figure of speech designed to emphasize a character's emotionally charged state. As a writer, it is important to recognize when you are using figurative language. Overused figures of speech become cliché and lose their ability to affect the reader as intended.

Imagery

- *The Scarlet Letter*, "Before this ugly edifice, and between it and the wheel-track of the street, was a grass plot, much overgrown with burdock, pigweed, apple peru, and such unsightly vegetation, which evidently found something congenial in the soil that had so early borne the black flower of civilized society, a prison. <u>But on one side of the portal, and rooted almost at the threshold, was a wild rosebush, covered, in this month of June, with its delicate gems, which might be imagined to offer their fragrance and fragile beauty to the prisoner as he went in, and to the condemned criminal as he came forth to his doom, in token that the deep heart of Nature could pity and be kind to him</u>" (pp. 33–34).

In "The Custom-House," the introductory essay that precedes *The Scarlet Letter*, Hawthorne distinguishes between novels and romances, calling his book an example of the latter. To describe a romance, he uses as an example the way moonlight subtly distorts a scene so that "all the details, so completely seen, are so spiritualized by the unusual light, that they seem to lose their actual substance, and become things of intellect" (p. 24). Rather than presenting details simply for the purpose of mimicking reality, Hawthorne uses physical details like the rosebush to show that even nature can "pity and be kind to" condemned criminals.

- *Johnny Tremain*, "She read the words in her halting manner: 'Let there be Lyte.'

And miraculously, as she stumbled over these words, there was light, for the sun came up out of the sea.

The children stood and looked at each other. The girl's face showed her excitement—and her fatigue. It was a pointed, sweet little face, her eyes a lighter brown than Isannah's and her hair not so strikingly pale.

Johnny whispered, 'Just like the sun coming up yonder out of the sea, pushing rays of light ahead of it'" (pp. 26–27).

Johnny and Cilla interpret the rising of the sun as symbolic because they are intent on studying the motto on Johnny's cup. To them, the coincidence of the sunrise and their conversation about the Lytes' motto means that Johnny is bound to have good fortune because of his relationship to the Lyte family. Later, the events of the book challenge Johnny and Cilla's assumption. In this way, the author uses a vivid detail about the sunrise to mislead readers and maintain an element of surprise.

Litotes

- *To Kill a Mockingbird*, "There is not a person in this courtroom who has never told a lie, who has never done an immoral thing, and there is no man living who has never looked upon a woman without desire" (p. 273).

Atticus could have stated his claim simply: every person in this courtroom has told a lie at some point and has done something immoral. His phrasing, using litotes, emphasizes that no man is free of guilt because it directly answers the unspoken argument, "But I would never do something like that!"

- *Narrative of the Life of Frederick Douglass*, "Indeed, it is not uncommon for slaves even to fall out and quarrel among themselves about the relative goodness of their masters, each contending for the superior goodness of his own over that of the others" (p. 12).

The author uses understatement to point out that slavery causes men to behave in ways that would typically be counterintuitive. Praising the kindness of someone who beats you ought to be uncommon, but thanks to the twisted logic of slavery, it has become common.

Metaphor

- *To Kill a Mockingbird*, "'Mockingbirds don't do one thing but make music for us to enjoy. They don't eat up people's gardens, don't nest in corncribs, they don't do one thing but sing their hearts out for us. That's why it's a sin to kill a mockingbird'" (p. 119).

- "'Well, it'd be sort of like shootin' a mockingbird, wouldn't it?'" (p. 370).

Some metaphors are used simply to describe a single character, place, or event. Others stand in for the entire concept of a book. A central metaphor of Harper Lee's novel, from which it takes its title, is the idea that killing mockingbirds is wrong. The two references quoted above are placed far apart in the book, so the reader must recall the earlier conversation in order to understand the later reference. Readers are left to figure out which characters are the "mockingbirds" and what actions would be the equivalent of shooting them.

- *The Sign of the Beaver*, "But this silence was different. It coiled around Matt and reached into his stomach to settle there in a hard knot" (p. 2).

As a reader, once you determine the **tenor** (the object described: silence) and the **vehicle** (the object used to describe it: a snake or a rope) of the metaphor, it is your task to figure out what message is conveyed by the comparison. In other words, if the silence is like a snake, what is a snake like? What is the author saying about this silence by comparing it to a snake? To answer this question, make a list of attributes that snakes and silence might possibly share. Snakes are poisonous (maybe); snakes are long and thin (probably not); snakes are sinister (perhaps); some snakes constrict things (more likely). From these characteristics, you can choose the meaning that best fits the context of the metaphor.

- "The Gift of the Magi," "Oh, and the next two hours tripped by on rosy wings. Forget the hashed metaphor. She was ransacking the stores for Jim's present" (*Words Aptly Spoken: American Literature*, p. 29).

A secondary, older meaning of the verb "to trip" is to walk lightly, skip, or frolic. Here, the author combines—and then acknowledges that he has combined—two different metaphors. To say that time "trips by" is to imagine time as a young child frolicking along a path, and it implies that time has feet. Children and animals that might be said to skip (lambs, puppies, horses) do not typically possess wings. To say that time passes "on rosy wings" is to imagine time as a bird or other flying creature. The two metaphors become muddled when mixed. As a writer, it is wise to use only one metaphor at a time.

Metonymy

- *Johnny Tremain*, "Everything was plentiful and well cooked. The kitchen was as clean or cleaner than many of those in the great houses. <u>Every member of the household had a clean shirt or petticoat</u>" (p. 9).

In an attempt to subtly convey information about a family's economic condition, an author may use a form of metonymy to show, rather than tell, their relative wealth. The author's statement that each member of the household had a clean shirt or petticoat stands in for an explicit claim that the Laphams are members of the working class. The technique also allows the author to demonstrate something about the way wealth was measured in a particular historical period. Today, you might say instead that someone belonged to a "one-car family" or went to the beach "once every four years."

- *The Witch of Blackbird Pond*, "'I say defy him!' came a hoarse shout. 'Nine train bands we have ready in Hartford county. Nigh unto a thousand men. <u>Let him look into a row of muskets</u> and he'll change his tune!'" (p. 155).

As the enraged colonists debate how to respond to the new regulations imposed on them by the king of England, one of them proposes a fight. He is not saying that a row of muskets leaning against a fence is particularly threatening. Instead, in this figure of speech, he uses the most salient object associated with soldiers—muskets—to stand in for the army he wants to deploy.

Onomatopoeia

- *The Sign of the Beaver*, "As he tramped through it he was accompanied by the <u>chirruping</u> of birds, the <u>chatter</u> of squirrels, and the <u>whine</u> and <u>twang</u> of thousands of bothersome insects. In the night he could recognize now the strange sounds that used to startle him. The <u>grunt</u> of a porcupine rummaging in the garden. The <u>boom</u> of the great horned owl" (p. 10).

Matt's nighttime walks through the forest, when sight is dimmed, are best represented through sounds. The author uses vivid words to represent the sounds of the wildlife, and many of the words are pronounced in a way that sounds similar to the noises that they represent. As an example, you might research the call of a great horned owl. The long double vowel in "boom" produces a similar sound. Likewise, the "wh" and "tw" in "whine" and "twang" make a whistling noise when spoken, comparable to the sound a mosquito makes when it circles your head.

- *An Old-Fashioned Girl*, "'Hi, there! Auster's coming!' shouted Tom, as he came <u>rattling</u> down the long, steep street outside the park.

They stepped aside, and he <u>whizzed</u> by, arms and legs going like mad, with the general appearance of a runaway engine" (pp. 57–58).

In this passage, the author attempts to mimic the sounds made by Tom's velocipede, an early bicycle made of wood or wrought iron with wooden wheels (sometimes called a "boneshaker" for that reason). The double "t" in "rattling" sounds like wood jarring against pavement. The double "z" in "whizzed" creates an extended hissing sound like that of a fast object passing a stationary one.

Parallelism

- *Up from Slavery*, "<u>It is important</u> and right that all <u>privileges</u> of the law be ours, but <u>it is vastly more important</u> that we be prepared for the exercises of these <u>privileges</u>. <u>The opportunity to earn a dollar</u> in a factory just now is worth infinitely more than <u>the opportunity to spend a dollar</u> in an opera house" (p. 109).

This passage contains two examples of parallelism. In the first case, the two clauses begin with the same statement, "It is important," but reverse the subject-object relationship from "privileges [should] be" to "we [should] be." In the second example, the two clauses begin with parallel noun phrases, "the opportunity to _____ a dollar," but the noun phrases use infinitives with opposite meanings ("to earn" and "to spend"). A helpful exercise when looking for parallelism in your own or others' writing is to diagram the sentence. Seeing the clauses visually can help you to identify parallelism.

- *Billy Budd*, "Invariably a proficient in his perilous calling, he was also more or less of a mighty boxer or wrestler. It was strength and beauty. Tales of his prowess were recited. <u>Ashore he was the champion; afloat the spokesman; on every suitable occasion always foremost</u>" (p. 2).

One benefit of parallelism, often seen in poetry, is that it permits the writer to leave off repeated elements of a sentence in subsequent clauses. In this compound sentence, only the first clause contains a subject and verb; however, all three independent clauses are understood to use the same core: "he was." The reader must recognize that the author is conserving space and words, and parallelism makes it easier for the reader to fill in the elided pieces of the sentence.

Personification

- *The Old Man and the Sea*, "Why did they make birds so delicate and fine as those sea swallows when the ocean can be so cruel? <u>She is kind and very beautiful. But she can be so cruel</u> and it comes so suddenly and such birds that fly, dipping and hunting, with their small sad voices are made too delicately for the sea" (p. 29).

Santiago, like many sailors, speaks of the ocean as if it were a woman, attributing human features to a part of nature. The old man goes on to explain that "[s]ome of the younger fisherman, those who used buoys as floats for their lines and had motorboats, bought when the shark livers had brought much money, spoke of her as *el mar* which is masculine. They spoke of her as a contestant or a place or even an enemy" (pp. 29–30). In this context, the old man's use of female personification is evidence of his love for the sea.

- *The Scarlet Letter*, "I found them growing on a grave which bore no tombstone, nor other memorial of the dead man, save <u>these ugly weeds that have taken upon themselves to keep him in remembrance</u>. They grew out of his heart, and typify, it may be, some hideous secret that was buried with him, and which he had done better to confess during his lifetime" (pp. 89–90).

In describing the weeds growing on an unmarked grave, the doctor attributes human agency and motivation to them, saying that they "have taken upon themselves" to memorialize the dead man. His subtler threat is that even if a man should take a secret to his grave, he is not safe from discovery: nature itself might reveal his crime.

Polysyndeton

- *The Witch of Blackbird Pond*, "All the land had to be sold, <u>and</u> the house <u>and</u> the slaves, <u>and</u> all the furniture from England. There wasn't anything left, not even enough for my passage" (p. 37).

Kit's sense of loss comes across strongly through the author's use of polysyndeton. Notice how the list moves from the broadest category (land), to a fixed location on the land (house), to the objects within the house (furniture). Arranging the objects in this order builds Kit's sense of despair that not only the largest things, but the smallest things as well, have been taken from her.

- *The Old Man and the Sea*, "I can remember the tail slapping and banging <u>and</u> the thwart breaking <u>and</u> the noise of the clubbing. I can remember you throwing me into the bow where the wet coiled lines were <u>and</u> feeling the whole boat shiver <u>and</u> the noise of you clubbing him like chopping a tree down <u>and</u> the sweet blood smell all over me" (p. 12).

Polysyndeton can be an effective device when a writer wishes to convey the rambling thoughts of a character, because it suggests that the speaker does not know when or how the sentence will end before he speaks it. As the boy pieces together his memories of the first time Santiago took him fishing, he does not know when he will reach the end of his memories, so he strings them together with multiple coordinating conjunctions, more than are grammatically necessary.

Rhyme

- *The Witch of Blackbird Pond*, "Two small heads bent earnestly over each of the three dog-eared primers which were all the dame school could boast.
  'That's fine,' praised Kit. 'Now go on.'
  'Love Christ <u>alway</u>,
  In secret <u>pray</u>,
  Mind little <u>play</u>,
  Make no <u>delay</u>,
  In doing good'" (p. 82).

Rhyme is not just a formal feature of poetry; it simplifies memorization, particularly for young children. Think about the ease with which you memorize nursery rhymes or popular rhyming songs. The dame school where Kit and Mercy teach, like many other one-room schoolhouses in early America, uses this technique in its primers.

- *"Paul Revere's Ride,"* "Listen my children and you shall <u>hear</u>
  Of the midnight ride of Paul <u>Revere</u>,
  On the eighteenth of April, in Seventy-<u>five</u>;
  Hardly a man is now <u>alive</u>
  Who remembers that famous day and <u>year</u>" (*Words Aptly Spoken: American Literature*, p. 73).

Rhyming poetry was used in early American schools to teach about important events in history. Memorizing the date "April 18, 1775" is made easier when you know that the year rhymes with the word "alive." This stanza uses the rhyme scheme AABBA. In other words, the first and second lines rhyme (designated "A"); the third and fourth lines rhyme (designated "B"), and the fifth line rhymes with the first two, so it is also marked "A." If you read further in Longfellow's poem, you will see that this rhyme scheme is not consistent, but the use of rhyme is maintained throughout the poem.

Simile

- *Narrative of the Life of Frederick Douglass*, "The competitors for this office sought as diligently to please their overseers, as the office-seekers in the political parties seek to please and deceive the people. The <u>same traits of character might be seen in Colonel Lloyd's slaves, as are seen in the slaves of the political parties</u>" (p. 8).

Simile can be used for political purpose, as the author does here. At a time when the equal humanity and equal rights of slaves were a subject of fierce debate, the author uses simile to compare black slaves to white politicians, asserting that they are, at least on one level, equals (in their hunger for advancement).

- *Born Again*, "With that he came around the desk and stood not six inches away, <u>like a baseball manager trying to provoke a fight with an umpire</u>. 'You make me sick,' he <u>roared</u>" (p. 118).

Colson uses a familiar sporting image, that of an angry baseball manager storming out to the plate and kicking dust in the face of a stoic referee, to give a sense of the explosive nature of his meeting with Senator Weicker.

Synecdoche

- *Up from Slavery*, "Nearly sixteen millions of <u>hands</u> will aid you in pulling the load upward, or they will pull against you the load downward" (p. 108).

Because Washington is speaking metaphorically about the ability of the black population to advance (pull the load upward) or detract from (pull downward) the growth of American society, he chooses to use the word "hands" to stand in for the men he is referencing.

- *Through Gates of Splendor*, "At any rate, the woman that had been cursed died within twenty-four hours. Her husband, brothers and father then felt duty bound to avenge her <u>blood</u> because the witch was as guilty as if he had shot her outright" (p. 71).

The Jivaros seeking revenge in the story were bound to avenge the woman's murder and the loss of her life, not the red fluid pumped by her heart, but because blood is closely associated with life, "her blood" is used to represent the woman's life as a whole.

For Further Reading

Greenholt, Jen, comp. and ed. *Words Aptly Spoken: American Literature.* 2nd ed. West End, NC: Classical Conversations MultiMedia, 2010.

Harmon, William, and Hugh Holman. *A Handbook to Literature.* 10th ed. Upper Saddle River, NJ: Pearson/Prentice Hall, 2006.

Kern, Andrew. *The Lost Tools of Writing: Level 1.* 4th ed. Concord, NC: The CiRCE Institute, 2011.

Richards, I. A. *The Philosophy of Rhetoric.* New York: Oxford UP, 1936.

Bibliography

Alcott, Louisa May. *An Old-Fashioned Girl*. New York, NY: Penguin Group, 2004. Print.

Colson, Charles. *Born Again*. Grand Rapids, MI: Chosen Books, 2008. Print.

Douglass, Frederick. *Narrative of the Life of Frederick Douglass, An American Slave*. New York: Dover Publications, 1995. Print.

Elliot, Elisabeth. *Through Gates of Splendor*. Wheaton, Ill.: Tyndale House Publishers, 2005. Print.

Forbes, Esther. *Johnny Tremain*. Boston: Houghton Mifflin Harcourt, 2011. Print.

Hawthorne, Nathaniel. *The Scarlet Letter*. New York: Dover Publications, 1994. Print.

Hemingway, Ernest. *The Old Man and the Sea*. New York: Scribner Paperback Fiction, 2003. Print.

Henry, O. "The Gift of the Magi." *Words Aptly Spoken: American Literature*. 2nd ed. Ed. Jen Greenholt. West End, NC: Classical Conversations MultiMedia, 2011.

---. "The Ransom of Red Chief." *Words Aptly Spoken: American Literature*. 2nd ed. Ed. Jen Greenholt. West End, NC: Classical Conversations MultiMedia, 2011.

Lee, Harper. *To Kill a Mockingbird*. New York: Warner Books, 1982.

London, Jack. *The Call of the Wild*. New York: Dover Publications, 1990. Print.

Longfellow, Henry Wadsworth. "Paul Revere's Ride." *Words Aptly Spoken: American Literature*. 2nd ed. Ed. Jen Greenholt. West End, NC: Classical Conversations MultiMedia, 2011.

---. "The Song of Hiawatha." *Words Aptly Spoken: American Literature*. 2nd ed. Ed. Jen Greenholt. West End, NC: Classical Conversations MultiMedia, 2011.

Mather, Cotton. *Essays to Do Good* (excerpt). *Words Aptly Spoken: American Literature*. 2nd ed. Ed. Jen Greenholt. West End, NC: Classical Conversations MultiMedia, 2011.

Melville, Herman. *Billy Budd, Sailor and Other Stories*. New York: Bantam Classics, 2006. Print.

Poe, Edgar Allan. *The Gold-Bug and Other Tales*. New York: Dover Publications, 1991. Print.

Speare, Elizabeth George. *The Sign of the Beaver*. New York: Houghton Mifflin Harcourt, 2011. Print.

---. *The Witch of Blackbird Pond*. New York: Houghton Mifflin Harcourt, 2011. Print.

Washington, Booker T. *Up From Slavery*. New York: Dover Publications, 1995.

Whitefield, George. "The Method of Grace." *Words Aptly Spoken: American Literature*. 2nd ed. Ed. Jen Greenholt. West End, NC: Classical Conversations MultiMedia, 2011.

Winthrop, John. "A Model of Christian Charity." *Words Aptly Spoken: American Literature*. 2nd ed. Ed. Jen Greenholt. West End, NC: Classical Conversations MultiMedia, 2011.

EXAMPLES FROM
Challenge II
LITERATURE

Examples from Challenge II Literature

Roman influence in England traces back to the first century AD, when the Romans invaded Britain. The Anglo-Saxons, whose rise followed the end of Roman rule, produced what are now known as some of the earliest works of literature in English. Classical influence was reinvigorated during the Renaissance as Englishmen had greater access to the world and looked to the ancients for inspiration. It is perhaps no wonder that British literature is replete with classical rhetorical figures and forms. This sample of classic British literature, from the Old English epic *Beowulf* to the twentieth-century biography *Something Beautiful for God*, will show you a wide range of styles and genres with varying degrees of classical influence.

All of these classic books are available in multiple editions, so unless you are using the same edition as the one cited in the bibliography, page numbers may not match precisely.

Alliteration

- *Beowulf*, "Often Scyld-Scefing wrested the mead-benches from troops of foes, from many tribes; he made fear fall upon the earls" (p. 1).

   An early function of rhyme was to make it easier for actors and bards (professional poets and entertainers) to memorize lines of poetry; however, Anglo-Saxon poetry like *Beowulf* did not use rhyme. Instead, one of the devices that made Anglo-Saxon poetry memorable was extensive alliteration. Most translations, even prose translations like the one above, attempt to keep this feature intact.

- *Sir Gawain and the Green Knight*, "Then the flowers come forth, meadows and groves are clad in green, the birds make ready to build, and sing sweetly for solace of the soft summer that follows thereafter" (p. 11).

   Notice the extensive use of alliteration in this passage. Both as a tool of memory and a garnish for poetic descriptions like this one, alliteration rolls smoothly off the tongue. Often, alliterative words come in pairs, such as a noun and a related adjective, or a noun and a related verb. When you see alliteration, look for patterns in the types of words used.

Allusion

- *Canterbury Tales*, "What? Should he study as a madman would

   Upon a book in cloister cell? Or yet

   Go labour with his hands and swink and sweat,

   As Austin bids? How shall the world be served?" (p. 6).

   The footnote for this passage indicates that "Austin" is a shortened version of "Augustine," referring to St. Augustine, the fourth-century convert to Christianity who founded an order of monks known to be sympathetic to the causes of common men. His followers had founded a monastery just outside of Canterbury in the early seventh century. By the fourteenth century, the Augustinian Order frequently came into conflict with other monastic orders over land, money, or favors from the nobility. Chaucer's narrator might be making a snide reference to the hypocrisy of these clashes, but on the level of character, he is setting up a contrast between his monk, who loves luxury and "new-world manners," and the Benedictine or Augustinian monks with their strict rules.

- *Out of the Silent Planet*, "They were quite unlike the horrors his imagination had conjured up, and for that reason had taken him off his guard. They appealed away from the Wellsian fantasies to an earlier, almost an infantile, complex of fears" (pp. 48–49).

H.G. Wells was a British author who wrote science fiction around the turn of the twentieth century. His famous 1898 novel *The War of the Worlds* describes an invasion of Earth by Martians. (American filmmaker Orson Welles adapted the novel as a radio drama in 1938; famously, some listeners did not realize that the story was fiction, causing panic and, later, outrage when the public recovered from the scare.) Wells's novel was highly influential in the genre of science fiction, so it is no surprise that Ransom would attribute his expectations about extraterrestrial life to this source.

Anaphora

✤ *Alice's Adventures in Wonderland*, "'What do you know about this business?' the King said to Alice.
'Nothing,' said Alice.
'Nothing whatever?' persisted the King.
'Nothing whatever,' said Alice" (p. 80).

Quick exchanges of dialogue often use a form of anaphora to indicate tension. Even though the answer has already been stated, the questioner continues to press the point, unsatisfied with the response he has been given. For the reader, the repeated word is drilled into his head until he, too, is ready to shout, "Enough!" Another rhetorical term that applies to this form of communication—a battle of words consisting of rapid-fire, alternating lines of banter—is **stichomythia**, from the Greek *stikhos* (row, line) + *mythos* (speech).

✤ "The Perishing of the Pendragons," "'Put a feather with a fossil and a bit of coral and everyone will thin[k] it's a specimen. Put the same feather with a ribbon and an artificial flower and everyone will think it's for a lady's hat. Put the same feather with an ink-bottle, a book, and a stack of writing paper, and most men will swear they've seen a quill pen. So you saw that map among tropic birds and shells and thought it was a map of Pacific Islands'" (p. 76).

When Father Brown is developing a theory or explaining a mystery to his companions, he uses multiple examples before telling them his point. By phrasing the examples in the same way, he eliminates as many variables as possible, helping his audience to focus in on the main point of the examples: the feather remains the same; only its environment changes, and with that, the way the feather is interpreted.

Antithesis

✤ *Out of the Silent Planet*, "Once or twice a small red creature scuttled across his path, but otherwise there seemed to be no life stirring in the wood; nothing to fear—except the fact of wandering unprovisioned and alone in a forest of unknown vegetation thousands or millions of miles beyond the reach or knowledge of man" (p. 48).

Antithesis can produce a kind of irony. Taken at face value, one statement, "wandering unprovisioned and alone," contradicts the other, that there is "nothing to fear." To reconcile these claims, the reader must recognize the underlying irony of the narrator's first observation. There seemed to be nothing to fear, but in fact, there was a great deal to fear.

✤ *A Tale of Two Cities*, "It was the best of times, it was the worst of times, it was the age of wisdom, it was the age of foolishness, it was the epoch of belief, it was the epoch of incredulity, it was the season of Light, it was the season of Darkness, it was the spring of hope, it was the winter of despair, we had everything before us, we had nothing before us, we were all going direct to Heaven, we are all going direct the other way—in short, the period was so far like the present period, that some of its noisiest authorities insisted on its being received, for good or for evil, in the superlative degree of comparison only" (p. 1).

Beyond the famous opening set, every pairing in this sentence represents antithesis. The author uses this device exhaustively in one sentence in order to demonstrate that the French Revolution was an age of contradiction.

Apostrophe

✤ *Paradise Lost*, "Of man's first disobedience, and the fruit
Of that forbidden tree, whose mortal taste
Brought death into the world, and all our woe,
With loss of Eden, till one greater Man
Restore us, and regain the blissful seat,
Sing Heav'nly Muse, that on the secret top
Of Oreb, or of Sinai, didst inspire" (pp. 3–4).

Examples from Challenge II Literature

If we simplify the syntax of this opening line, it reads, "Sing, Heavenly Muse, about man's first disobedience and the fruit of the forbidden tree." Like a classic Greek or Roman epic, Milton's poem begins with an invocation of the muse, but because he is writing a Christian epic, his muse is the Holy Spirit, who inspired Moses to write the Pentateuch.

- *Alice's Adventures in Wonderland*, "'I hope they'll remember her saucer of milk at tea-time. <u>Dinah, my dear</u>! I wish you were down here with me! There are no mice in the air, I'm afraid, but you might catch a bat, and that's very like a mouse, you know'" (p. 3).

A playful book like *Alice's Adventures in Wonderland* is full of rhetorical devices. Here, Alice is falling down the rabbit hole, very much alone, but she speaks to her cat, Dinah, as if the animal were present and could hear her. In doing so, she directs the reader's attention back to the world she has left, and the author provides the reader with a small amount of background information about Alice.

Assonance

- *Sir Gawain and the Green Knight*, "Now are the praise and the ren<u>ow</u>n of the R<u>ou</u>nd Table overthrown by one man's speech, since all keep silence for dread ere ever they have seen a blow!" (p. 6).

This passage is a good lesson in the differences between modern and Middle English pronunciation. The Middle English vowel "o" is pronounced long, as in the word "note." As a result, "now" and "blow" would be true rhymes in medieval pronunciation, where in modern English they are "eye rhymes" (they appear to rhyme but are not pronounced accordingly). Likewise, in Middle English, "ou" and "ow" are both pronounced like the word "boot." The words "renown" and "round," then, demonstrate assonance.

- *Paradise Lost*, "So spake the apostate Angel, though in <u>pain</u>,
Vaunting aloud, but racked with deep <u>despair</u>:
And him thus answered soon his bold compeer" (p. 6).

"Pain" and "despair" do not rhyme—their final consonants differ—but their accented syllables share a common vowel sound. In that way, Milton does not use precise rhyme, but he does create a rhythmic, elegant sound within the structure of his poem.

Asyndeton

- *A Passage to India*, "He was excited partly by his wrongs, but much more by the knowledge that someone sympathized with them. It was this that led him to <u>repeat</u>, <u>exaggerate</u>, <u>contradict</u>. She had proved her sympathy by criticizing her fellow-countrywoman to him, but even earlier he had known" (p. 21).

The frenzied pace of Dr. Aziz's thoughts is made manifest in his way of speaking. The caution with which he initially speaks is replaced with a flood of words. In this example, asyndeton is one sign of his excitement, because it suggests that he does all three of these things—repeat, exaggerate, and contradict—at the same time rather than sequentially.

- *Animal Farm*, "And then, after a few preliminary tries, the whole farm burst out into *Beasts of England* in tremendous unison. <u>The cows lowed it, the dogs whined it, the sheep bleated it, the horses whinnied it, the ducks quacked it</u>" (p. 13).

When the animals of Manor Farm come together to sing their anthem of rebellion, the author uses asyndeton to indicate that the examples he has given (cows, dogs, sheep, horses, and ducks) do not represent a complete list of the animals present. The reader must add to this list in his imagination to get a full picture of the spirit of rebellion. Asyndeton also gives the reader a sense that everything is happening at once, full of energy and cacophony.

Chiasmus

- *Alice's Adventures in Wonderland*, "The Fish-Footman began by producing from under his arm a great letter, nearly as large as himself, and this he handed over to the other, saying, in a solemn tone, '<u>For the Duchess</u>. An invitation <u>from the Queen</u> to play croquet.' The Frog-Footman repeated, in the same solemn tone, only changing the order of the words a little, '<u>From the Queen</u>. An invitation <u>for the Duchess</u> to play croquet'" (pp. 36–37).

This scene uses a subtle form of chiasmus to create humor. The two footmen are ridiculous in part because they are attempting to accomplish the same task. On the other hand, the scene also illustrates—as many of the scenes in *Alice* do—one of the peculiarities of the English language: even though the language is not as highly inflected as a language like Latin, word order can still be manipulated without changing the meaning of the sentence.

- ❂ *The Pilgrim's Progress*, "The pathway was here also exceeding narrow, and therefore good Christian was the more put to it; for <u>when he sought in the dark to shun the ditch on the one hand, he was ready to tip over into the mire</u> on the other; also <u>when he sought to escape the mire, without great carefulness, he would be ready to fall into the ditch</u>" (p. 67).

Chiasmus is effective in portraying no-win situations, when a character finds himself figuratively or literally "between a rock and a hard place." In this example, Christian must pass between the ditch and the mire without stumbling into either. When he tries to steer away from one, he inevitably slips closer to the other. The author uses chiasmus to heighten the sense of Christian's danger.

Consonance

- ❂ *Sir Gawain and the Green Knight*, "And if ye <u>will</u> listen to me, but for a little <u>while</u>, I <u>will</u> tell it even as it stands in my story stiff and strong, fixed in the letter, as it hath long been known in the land" (p. 1).

Sir Gawain is an excellent example of the diverse devices used in Middle English poetry, which can be read in the original form even by those who have not studied Middle English extensively. This prose translation preserves many of those features, including alliteration and consonance, both present in this passage. "Will" and "While" demonstrate consonance because they contain the same consonant sounds, separated by different vowel sounds. All of these tools make the poem more memorable, both for the bard telling it and for the audience listening.

- ❂ *The Hobbit*, "As he lay in bed he could hear Thorin still humming to himself in the best bedroom next to him:

    Far over the <u>misty</u> <u>mountains</u> cold
    To dungeons deep and caverns old
    We must away, ere break of day,
    To find our long-forgotten gold" (p. 27).

The dwarves' poem is characterized by a rhyme scheme of AABA: the first two and the last lines of each four-line stanza rhyme. In addition to the rhyme at the end of the lines, some lines demonstrate internal rhyme, assonance, consonance, or alliteration. In this example, "misty" and "mountain" do not have the same vowel sounds, but the dominant consonant sounds "m" and "t" are the same.

Epistrophe

- ❂ *Animal Farm*, "The general feeling on the farm was well expressed in a poem entitled *Comrade Napoleon*, which was composed by Minimus and which ran as follows:

    Friend of fatherless!
    Fountain of happiness!
    Lord of the swill-bucket! Oh, how my soul is on
    Fire when I gaze at thy
    Calm and commanding eye,
    Like the sun in the sky,
    <u>*Comrade Napoleon!*</u>

    Thou art the giver of
    All that thy creatures love,
    Full belly twice a day, clean straw to roll upon;
    Every beast great or small
    Sleeps at peace in his stall,
    Thou watchest over all,
    <u>*Comrade Napoleon!*</u>" (p. 94).

Patriotic songs like this one often incorporate some type of refrain or repeated line that is memorable and emphatic, meant to stir the emotions of listeners and inspire them. *Animal Farm* illustrates the reason for this principle. The sheep and other less intelligent animals cannot remember the full content of the Seven Commandments, so they memorize "Four legs good, two legs bad." Likewise, listeners might not remember the entire poem, but the most important chant—"Comrade Napoleon"—might linger in their minds.

- *The Hobbit*, "O! What are you seeking,
    And where are you making?
    The faggots are reeking,
    The bannocks are baking!
    O! tril-lil-lil-lolly
    the valley is jolly,
    <u>ha! ha!</u>

    O! Where are you going
    With beards all a-wagging?

No knowing, no knowing
What brings Mister Baggins,
And Balin and Dwalin
down into the valley
in June
<u>*ha! ha!*</u>" (p. 48).

To make his fantasy world more realistic, the author creates a distinct culture for each of the races in his novel. The elves' poetry is different from that of the dwarves, although both incorporate rhyme. It is more playful, using refrains and repeated lines like "ha! ha!" in the sample poem. As a writer, if you create an imaginary world, details such as forms of poetry and colloquial expressions can add texture and bring your world to life.

Foreshadowing

- *The Pilgrim's Progress*, "<u>The gentleman's name that met him was Mr. Worldly Wiseman</u>: he dwelt in the town of Carnal Policy, a very great Town, and also hard by from whence Christian came" (p. 21).

One of the most explicit forms of foreshadowing can be found in allegories, which use characters and places to represent bigger ideas. Even if the reader has no context in which to place a new character, the character's name often reveals something about him or her. In this example from *The Pilgrim's Progress*, we meet "Mr. Worldly Wiseman" and can immediately deduce his role in the plot, based only on his name.

- *A Tale of Two Cities*, "It is likely enough that, rooted in the woods of France and Norway, there were growing trees, when that sufferer was put to death, <u>already marked by the Woodman, Fate</u>, to come down and be sawn into boards, to make <u>a certain movable framework</u> with a sack and a knife in it, terrible in history" (p. 6).

In this passage early in *A Tale of Two Cities*, Dickens refers to trees that are "already marked by…Fate" to become "a certain movable framework with a sack and a knife." This not-so-subtle reference to the guillotine that killed many during the French Revolution foreshadows the violence that will emerge later in the novel.

Hyperbole

- *A Passage to India*, "And pointing about the room he peopled it with clerks and officials, all benevolent because they lived long ago. 'So <u>we would sit giving for ever</u>—on a carpet instead of chairs, that is the chief change between now and then, but <u>I think we would never punish anyone</u>'" (p. 74).

Talking about the problems of the present can drive us to develop an overly romantic view of the past. In this example, Dr. Aziz imagines a history for the eighteenth-century building in which Mr. Fielding now lives. He uses superlative words such as "for ever" and "never" to describe that era, even though he and the reader know that no period of human history has been perfect, in order to create a contrast with the unjust social practices of the present age.

- *Something Beautiful for God*, "When the train began to move, and I walked away, <u>I felt as though I were leaving behind me all the beauty and all the joy in the universe</u>" (p. 17).

The author does not literally believe that there is nothing left of beauty in the world when he leaves Mother Teresa's side, but he uses this form of exaggeration in an attempt to convey how compelling this woman's presence is.

Imagery

- *Sir Gawain and the Green Knight*, "<u>Then they brought him his shield, which was of bright red, with the pentangle painted thereon in gleaming gold</u>. And why that noble prince bare the pentangle I am minded to tell you, though my tale tarry thereby. It is a sign that Solomon set ere-while, as betokening truth; for it is a figure with five points and each line overlaps the other, and nowhere hath it beginning or end, so that in English it is called 'the endless knot.' And therefore was it well suiting to this knight and to his arms, since Gawain was faithful in five and five-fold, for pure was he as gold, void of all villainy, and endowed with all virtues" (p. 13).

One defining feature of epic poetry is its detailed descriptions of the hero's armor and weaponry. These descriptions are often full of understated imagery. Some poets use imagery without explaining its meaning, as a way of subtly demonstrating some feature of the hero's character. For example, other poets might stop after "painted thereon in gleaming gold." It would be up to the reader to ask what a pentangle is and why it was significant. By contrast, to ensure that the reader understands why the pentangle is appropriate, this poet goes on to explain exactly why Gawain bears that symbol.

- *Jane Eyre*, "But what had befallen the night? The moon was not yet set, and we were all in shadow: I could scarcely see my master's face, near as I was. And what ailed the chestnut tree? it writhed and groaned; while wind roared in the laurel walk, and came sweeping over us" (p. 240).

Jane and Mr. Rochester first embrace one another under the spreading boughs of the old chestnut tree, and Jane notices the way the branches tremble in the wind. As soon as Jane accepts Mr. Rochester's proposal, the tree begins to writhe and groan, mimicking the tone of the scene and foreshadowing what is to come. Mr. Rochester comments that the weather is changing, but the reader recognizes that the tree is representative of the mood of the novel. That night, it is struck by lightning, and "half of it [is] split away" (p. 241).

Litotes

- *Pride and Prejudice*, "'You saw me dance at Meryton, I believe, sir.'

  'Yes, indeed, and received no inconsiderable pleasure from the sight. Do you often dance at St. James's?'" (p. 16).

The double negative in Sir William Lucas's comment is a polite way to say that Mr. Darcy is, in fact, a good dancer and a considerable pleasure to watch. This type of understatement is often present in novels about polite society, when compliments must be dressed in formal language to be considered proper.

- *Something Beautiful for God*, "The Corporation receives a good deal of criticism one way and another, most of it deserved. I have not been backward myself in joining in" (p. 36).

The author means to say that he has been an active member of those who criticize the BBC, but he chooses to phrase this statement by negating its opposite, showing readers that he does not, although he could, exempt himself from this group of people. This is a demonstration of honesty, because he chooses to reveal information that might portray him as a hypocrite.

Metaphor

- *Paradise Lost*, "…I thence
  Invoke thy aid to my advent'rous song,
  That with no middle flight intends to soar
  Above th' Aonian mount, while it pursues
  Things unattempted yet in prose or rhyme" (p. 4).

The "Aonian mount" refers to the home of the classical Muses, about whom Homer and Virgil wrote in their epics *The Iliad*, *The Odyssey*, and *The Aeneid*. The author describes his poem as a song, but speaks of it as though it were a bird that could soar over mountains.

- *A Passage to India*, "He said stiffly, 'I do not consider Mrs. Moore my friend, I only met her accidentally in my mosque,' and was adding 'a single meeting is too short to make a friend,' but before he could finish the sentence the stiffness vanished from it, because he felt Fielding's fundamental good will. His own went out to it, and grappled beneath the shifting tides of emotion which can alone bear the voyager to an anchorage but may also carry him across it on to the rocks. He was safe really—as safe as the shore-dweller who can only understand stability and supposes that every ship must be wrecked, and he had sensations the shore-dweller cannot know" (p. 70).

The author uses several types of figurative language in this passage, but the dominant metaphor is of a shore-dwelling sailor or ship that goes out to meet a voyager and help him make it safely to shore. Emotion, the metaphor says, is like the tide. Sailors need the tide in order to sail, but the tide can also work against them. Likewise, emotion is necessary

Examples from Challenge II Literature

for healthy interactions, but in excess it can destroy relationships between men.

Metonymy

- *Paradise Lost*, "…Him the Almighty Power
  Hurled headlong flaming from the ethereal sky,
  With hideous ruin and combustion down
  To bottomless perdition, there to dwell
  In adamantine chains and penal fire,
  Who durst defy the Omnipotent to <u>arms</u>" (p. 4).

"Arms," or armaments, refers to weapons or ammunition. The author is not saying that the Serpent (Satan) drove God toward a stash of weapons; rather, he means that Satan defied God to the point that God declared war against Satan. Because armaments are central to the ability to wage war, authors can speak of "arms" and readers understand that they are using a closely associated object to stand in for the larger concept of war.

- *A Tale of Two Cities*, "France, less favoured on the whole as to matters spiritual than <u>her sister of the shield and trident</u>, rolled with exceeding smoothness down hill, making paper money and spending it" (p. 2).

The symbol of Great Britain, pictured on early English coins, is a woman wearing a helmet and carrying a shield and a trident. Known as Britannia since the time of the Romans, this figure would have appeared on art and coinage from both the era of the French Revolution and that of Dickens. Rather than stating that France was less favored than England, the author allows the closely associated symbol of Britannia to stand in for the nation.

Onomatopoeia

- *Animal Farm*, "The two horses had just lain down when a brood of ducklings, which had lost their mother, filed into the barn, <u>cheeping</u> feebly and wandering from side to side to find some place where they would not be trodden on" (p. 5).

Animal noises are often named by the sound they make, in a form of onomatopoeia. When you say the word "cheep" repeatedly, the pronunciation is very similar to the sound that ducklings or chicks make. Other examples would be the words "quack," "moo," and "caw."

- *The Hobbit*, "The <u>yells</u> and <u>yammering</u>, <u>croaking</u>, <u>jibbering</u> and <u>jabbering</u>; <u>howls</u>, <u>growls</u> and curses; <u>shrieking</u> and <u>skriking</u>, that followed were beyond description. Several hundred wild cats and wolves being roasted slowly alive together would not have compared with it" (p. 64).

Most readers of *The Hobbit* have probably not spent time in a cavern with a hoard of goblins. When describing an invented (particularly a frightening) race of creatures like goblins, normal sound effects may not be sufficient to bring the scene to life. In this example, the author uses a series of words that are pronounced like the sound they represent. Together, these sounds allow the author to create a realistic description of an unfamiliar scene.

Parallelism

- *Out of the Silent Planet*, "In less than a minute <u>he was climbing</u> out onto dry land again. <u>He was running</u> up a steep incline. And now <u>he was running</u> through purple shadow between the stems of another forest of the huge plants" (p. 47).

These three sentences demonstrate parallel structure. Each verb is in the past imperfect tense, formed by combining a past-tense linking verb ("was") with a present participle ("–ing"). Presenting these three actions one after the other shows forward movement. The three actions seem to be taking place simultaneously rather than in sequence, so Ransom's flight seems swifter.

- *Something Beautiful for God*, "<u>I ran away and stayed away; Mother Teresa moved in and stayed</u>. That was the difference. She, a nun, rather slightly built, with a few rupees in her pocket; not particularly clever, or particularly gifted in the arts of persuasion" (p. 22).

The author uses a parallel structure to draw a contrast in his own behavior and that of Mother

Teresa. He ran away, and she moved in. He stayed away, and she stayed. A semicolon, which separates two independent clauses, is often used in combination with this type of parallel structure.

Personification

- *Alice's Adventures in Wonderland*, "Alice sighed wearily. 'I think you might do something better with the time,' she said, 'than wasting it in asking riddles that have no answers.'

  <u>'If you knew Time as well as I do,'</u> said the Hatter, 'you wouldn't talk about wasting *it*. It's *him*.'

  'I don't know what you mean,' said Alice" (p. 46).

  Alice and the Mad Hatter misunderstand each other because he is using personification and she is not. The Mad Hatter thinks and speaks of Time (capital 't') as though time were a human being and a friend; Alice thinks and speaks of time (lowercase 't') as an abstract concept. She does not realize that she is, nonetheless, using figurative language when she speaks of "wasting time" and "beating time," so the Mad Hatter uses personification to call attention to the fact that even her sane use of language is not as straightforward as she believes.

- *Jane Eyre*, "…sometimes on a sunny day it began even to be pleasant and genial, and a greenness grew over those brown beds, which, freshening daily, suggested the thought that <u>Hope traversed them at night, and left each morning brighter traces of her steps</u>" (p. 72).

  In this fanciful description, Jane imagines "hope" as a woman who walks through the bare plots of ground in spring and leaves behind budding flowers instead of footprints.

Polysyndeton

- *Sir Gawain and the Green Knight*, "And another custom he had also, that came of his nobility, that he would never eat upon an high day till he had been advised of some knightly deed, or some strange and marvelous tale, <u>of his ancestors, or of arms, or of other ventures</u>" (p. 2).

  This example of polysyndeton shows an open-ended list: the tales that could be told to the king were numerous, and as a result, so were the tales that the poet could tell. How convenient! Furthermore, oral poetry is a unique form, because the bard performing the piece might modify the poem each time he told it, changing small particulars to suit his audience or adding detail as he went along. For this reason, polysyndeton is particularly suitable for written versions of oral poetry.

- *Pride and Prejudice*, "'But, however, he did not admire her at all; indeed, nobody can, you know; and he seemed quite struck with Jane as she was going down the dance. She <u>he inquired</u> who she was, <u>and got introduced, and asked</u> her for the two next. Then the two third he danced with Miss King, <u>and the two fourth with Maria Lucas, and the two fifth with Jane</u> again, <u>and the two sixth with Lizzy, and the Boulanger</u>—'" (p. 8).

  In her excitement about the prospect of marrying one of her girls to Mr. Bingley, Mrs. Bennet uses conjunctions with abandon, scattering them throughout her sentences. The effect is to give the reader no indication if or when the list is about to end. Appropriately, Mrs. Bennet's commentary is interrupted by her husband, who is wondering the same thing.

Rhyme

- *Canterbury Tales*, "When April with his showers sweet with <u>fruit</u>

  The drought of March has pierced unto the <u>root</u>

  And bathed each vein with liquor that has <u>power</u>

  To generate therein and sire the <u>flower</u>…" ("The General Prologue," p. 1).

  Most of Chaucer's *Canterbury Tales* is written in rhyming couplets (pairs of lines). This is a modern English translation. The Middle English can be difficult to read, but it is possible for those who have not studied Middle English extensively to understand what is being said. Compare the two versions, and you will notice that the translator has restructured some of the poem's lines in order to preserve the rhyming structure. Some of the rhymes are simple rhymes, like "fruit" and "root," while other are more complex two-syllable rhymes such as "power" and "flower."

- *The Pilgrim's Progress*, "When at the first I took my pen in <u>hand</u>

  Thus for to write; I did not under<u>stand</u>

Examples from Challenge II Literature

That I at all should make a little <u>book</u>
In such a mode; nay, I had under<u>took</u>
To make another, which when almost <u>done</u>,
Before I was aware, I this be<u>gun</u>" (p. 5).

Like other books of its period, *The Pilgrim's Progress* begins with a prologue, called an "apology," which is written in rhyming couplets (pairs of lines). The book itself is written in prose. The apology was an opportunity for the author to anticipate critiques of his work on a political, theological, or artistic basis and to present himself as a humble and unassuming person.

Simile

- *Alice's Adventures in Wonderland*, "'I'm better now—but I'm a deal too flustered to tell you—all I know is, something comes at me <u>like a Jack-in-the-box</u>, and up I goes <u>like a sky-rocket</u>!'" (p. 23).

Often, we use similes to describe a new or unusual experience. Bill the lizard encounters a giant Alice and is sent flying out of the White Rabbit's house. He has never experienced this before, so he turns to familiar images—a Jack-in-the-box and a skyrocket—to describe the unknown occurrence.

- "The Blue Cross," "Between the silver ribbon of morning and the green glittering ribbon of sea, the boat touched Harwich and <u>let loose a swarm of folk like flies</u>, among whom the man we must follow was by no means conspicuous—nor wished to be" (p. 1).

The author does not explicitly tell readers that the morning was like a ribbon of silver and the sea was like one of green, but he does make a specific comparison between the people leaving the boat and a swarm of flies. Readers can picture a hovering cloud of black insects emerging from a small opening and filling the space outside, so it is easy to imagine the crowd jostling and pushing one another as they exit the boat, moving en masse in such a way that it would be difficult to separate one face from the crowd.

Synecdoche

- *A Passage to India*, "'Oh, oh, who is that?' said <u>a nervous and respectful voice</u>; he could not remember where he had heard its tones before" (p. 346).

Readers know that Dr. Aziz is not hearing a disembodied voice; some person is speaking to him. However, because the doctor does not see the newcomer immediately, he refers to him as a "voice," allowing that part of the newcomer's identity, the most important characteristic at this point, to stand in for the person as a whole.

- *The Screwtape Letters*, "You want to lean pretty heavily on those neighbours. Make his mind flit to and fro between an expression like 'the body of Christ' and the actual <u>faces</u> in the next pew. It matters very little, of course, what kind of people that next pew really contains" (p. 6).

Writers often refer to unnamed characters as "faces," substituting this part for the body as a whole. One reason might be that we often notice a person's face before anything else, and we assume that the personality and character of an individual is most visible in the face. In your own writing, consider how you introduce new characters, and what parts of their bodies you use to stand in for the whole person. These decisions are not trivial, because they affect the focus of your reader's attention.

For Further Reading

Greenholt, Jennifer, comp. and ed. *Words Aptly Spoken: British Literature*. 2nd ed. West End, NC: Classical Conversations MultiMedia, 2010.

Harmon, William, and Hugh Holman. *A Handbook to Literature*. 10th ed. Upper Saddle River, NJ: Pearson/Prentice Hall, 2006.

Kern, Andrew. *The Lost Tools of Writing: Level 1*. 4th ed. Concord, NC: The CiRCE Institute, 2011.

Richards, I. A. *The Philosophy of Rhetoric*. New York: Oxford UP, 1936.

Examples from Challenge II Literature

Bibliography

Austen, Jane. *Pride and Prejudice*. New York: Dover, 1995.

Beowulf. Dover Thrift edition. Tran. R. K. Gordon. Mineola, NY: Dover, 1992.

Brontë, Charlotte. *Jane Eyre*. Mineola, NY: Dover Publications, 2002.

Bunyan, John. *The Pilgrim's Progress*. Mineola, NY: Dover Publications, 2003.

Carroll, Lewis. *Alice's Adventures in Wonderland*. Illus. John Tenniel. New York: Dover, 1993.

Chaucer, Geoffrey. *Selected Canterbury Tales*. Dover Thrift edition. Tran. J. U. Nicolson. Ed. Candace Ward. Mineola, NY: Dover Publications, 1994.

Chesterton, G. K. "The Blue Cross." *Favorite Father Brown Stories*. New York: Dover Publications, 1993. Print.

---. "The Perishing of the Pendragons." *Favorite Father Brown Stories*. New York: Dover Publications, 1993. Print.

Defoe, Daniel. *Robinson Crusoe*. Mineola, NY: Dover Publications, 1998.

Dickens, Charles. *A Tale of Two Cities*. Mineola, NY: Dover Publications, 1999.

Forster, E. M. *A Passage to India*. San Diego: Harcourt Brace Jovanovich, 1984.

Lewis, C. S. *Out of the Silent Planet*. New York: Scribner, 2003.

---. *The Screwtape Letters: Screwtape Proposes a Toast*. San Francisco: HarperOne, 2009.

Milton, John. *Paradise Lost*. Mineola, NY: Dover Publications, 2005.

Muggeridge, Malcolm. *Something Beautiful for God: Mother Teresa of Calcutta*. San Francisco: HarperOne, 1986.

Orwell, George. *Animal Farm*. New York, NY: Signet Classics, 1996.

Peters, Ellis. *A Morbid Taste for Bones*. New York: Grand Central, 1994.

Sir Gawain and the Green Knight. Tran. Jessie L. Weston. New York: Dover Publications, 2003.

Swift, Jonathan. *Gulliver's Travels*. Mineola, NY: Dover Publications, 1996.

Tolkien, J. R. R. *The Hobbit*. Rev. ed. New York: Ballantine Books, 1986.

EXAMPLES FROM

Challenge III

LITERATURE

Examples from Challenge III Literature

The Renaissance ("re-birth") in Europe brought with it a renewed fascination with classical Greek and Roman culture, including classical oratory and performance. William Shakespeare's plays provide fertile material for rhetorical studies of all kinds. The plays were performed at the English court and in the presence of theater patrons, on whose generosity and approval the whole company's livelihood depended, so the author had to dance through complex choreography, combining political correctness, sly literary wit, and the slapstick humor demanded by the general public.

Alone or in collaboration, Shakespeare (1564–1616) wrote more than thirty-five plays, over a hundred sonnets, and four additional works of poetry. He coined dozens of new words or variations on older words, including the now familiar "lackluster," "gossip" (verb), and "eyeball." He also demonstrated his familiarity with a wide vocabulary of rhetorical techniques derived from Aristotle's *Rhetoric* and popularized in English through Thomas Wilson's *The Arte of Rhetorique*. As a result, you will find an abundance of examples beyond those quoted here for each literary device covered in this study aid.

All of Shakespeare's plays are available in multiple editions, so unless you are using the same edition as the one cited in the bibliography, page numbers may not match precisely.

Alliteration

- *Henry V*, "I see you stand like greyhounds in the
   slips,
     Straining upon the start. The game's afoot.
     Follow your spirit, and upon this charge
     Cry, 'God for Harry! England and Saint George!'"
     (3.1.34–37).

   Henry's famous inspirational speech to the English troops outside of Harfleur employs a number of rhetorical techniques. In this passage, notice that although the lines do not rhyme, the final stressed consonant in each line alliterates loosely with the first stressed consonant in the next line. Alliteration gives continuity to the speech without losing the punch or rhythm of the individual lines.

- *Macbeth*, "And oftentimes, to win us to our harm,
     The instruments of darkness tell us truths,
     Win us with honest trifles, to betray 's
     In deepest consequence—" (1.3.135–138).

   Banquo cautions Macbeth against believing the witches' prophecies because they may lie subtly, beginning with a truth and then twisting it. The alliteration in this passage adds another layer to the way truth can be turned into trifles, and then into betrayal.

Allusion

- *Hamlet*, "…Oh, it offends me to the
     soul to hear a robustious periwig-pated fellow tear a passion to tatters, to very rags, to split the ears of the groundlings, who for the most part are capable of nothing but inexplicable dumbshows and noise. I would have such a fellow whipped for o'erdoing Termagant;
     it out-Herods Herod. Pray you, avoid it"
     (3.2.8–15).

   As Hamlet gives instructions to the troupe of players before they perform in front of the king and queen, he names Herod as a negative example. His allusion could be to either of two Herods named in the Bible: Herod the Great, who ordered the death of the infants at the time of Jesus's birth, or Herod Antipas, who beheaded John the Baptist and ordered the death of Christ. More likely, Hamlet alludes to the actors who played Herod the Great in the medieval "mystery plays" chronicling the life of Christ, who had rendered Herod a notorious and familiar villain. In fact, just a few years later (1613), Elizabeth Cary would write a play (*The Tragedy of Mariam*) based on Herod the Great's second wife.

- *Macbeth*, "...The merciless Macdonwald
    (Worthy to be a rebel, for to that
    The multiplying villanies of nature
    Do swarm upon him) from the Western Isles
    Of <u>kerns</u> and <u>gallowglasses</u> is supplied..." (1.2.11–15).

The sergeant describes the battle in colloquial terms used to reference Ireland and Scotland. "Kern" refers to a lightly armed Gaelic foot soldier, while "gallowglass" is another term for a Scottish horseman armed with axes and serving under the Irish. These medieval terms are used to lend authenticity to Shakespeare's play.

Anaphora

- *Henry V*, "…Therefore, you men of Harfleur,
    Take pity of your town and of your people
    <u>Whiles yet</u> my soldiers are in my command,
    <u>Whiles yet</u> the cool and temperate wind of grace
    O'erblows the filthy and contagious clouds
    Of heady murder, spoil, and villany" (3.3.27–32).

Forms of repetition such as anaphora allow a speaker to reiterate his or her central point while adding extra detail or examples. In King Henry's speech before the gates of Harfleur, his first statement refers to a concrete condition ("whiles yet my soldiers are in my command"); the second paints a metaphorical picture ("whiles yet the cool and temperate wind of grace o'erblows the filthy and contagious clouds of heady murder, spoil and villany"). In this way, Henry uses repetition to intensify his threats and remind the French inhabitants that they have only a little time remaining in which to sue for mercy.

- *Hamlet*, "An earnest conjuration from the King,
    <u>As England was</u> his faithful tributary,
    <u>As love between them</u> like the palm might flourish,
    <u>As peace should still</u> her wheaten garland wear
    And stand a comma 'tween their amities,
    And many suchlike 'as'es of great charge,
    That on the view and knowing of these contents,
    Without debatement further, more or less,
    He should those bearers put to sudden death,
    Not shriving time allowed" (5.2.43–52).

The letter Hamlet describes begins in the same way that most governmental resolutions begin today: by laying out the current conditions that have led to the resolution or request. Today, lawmakers use the word "whereas," but Hamlet uses the simpler form "as," meaning "because" or "since." Because England was Denmark's faithful tributary and peace had an obligation to wear her garland, the king of England should put to death the bearers of this letter.

Antithesis

- *Hamlet*, "Therefore our sometime sister, now our queen,
    Th' imperial jointress to this warlike state,
    Have we (as 'twere with a <u>defeated joy</u>—
    With <u>an auspicious and a dropping</u> eye,
    With <u>mirth in funeral</u> and with <u>dirge in marriage</u>,
    In equal scale weighing <u>delight and dole</u>)
    Taken to wife…." (1.2.8–14).

In this speech, Claudius demonstrates excellent use of antithesis. The king, his brother, has recently died, and Claudius must announce his decision to wed the queen. To prevent angering his new subjects, he must find a way to set side by side "delight and dole." He uses the device of antithesis to present himself as, simultaneously, a grieving brother and a celebratory bridegroom.

- *Julius Caesar*, "Will you be patient? Will you stay awhile?
    I have o'ershot myself to tell you of it.
    I fear I wrong <u>the honorable men</u>
    <u>Whose daggers have stabbed Caesar</u>; I do fear it" (3.2.161–164).

Rather than accusing the conspirators of being evil murderers, Antony praises them, wisely allowing the mob to identify the paradox in what he says. He calls Brutus an honorable man and also one whose dagger stabbed Caesar. This seeming contradiction keeps Antony safe while at the same time achieving his goal: turning the mob against the conspirators.

Apostrophe

- *Hamlet*, "Or that the Everlasting had not fixed
  His canon 'gainst self-slaughter! <u>Oh, God, God</u>,
  How weary, stale, flat, and unprofitable
  Seem to me all the uses of this world!"
  (1.2.135–138).

Hamlet's agony over his mother's infidelity to his father's memory leads him to cry out to God. One theatrical rendering of this speech might present Hamlet looking up at this point as though addressing God directly. Either way, he calls on a higher judge in the matter, pointing the audience's eyes upward as well.

- *Julius Caesar*, "So vile a thing as Caesar! But, <u>O grief</u>,
  Where hast thou led me? I perhaps speak this
  Before a willing bondman; then I know
  My answer must be made. But I am armed,
  And dangers are to me indifferent" (1.3.115–119).

Cassius tests Casca's loyalties before inviting him to join the plot. In the meantime, he shrugs off some of the responsibility for what he is about to say by pointing Casca's eyes to another authority, grief. He personifies this abstract concept and speaks as though it were another party present in the conversation.

Assonance

- *Hamlet*, "Who would fardels bear,
  To grunt and <u>sweat</u> under a weary life,
  But that the <u>dread</u> of something after <u>death</u>,
  The undiscovered country from whose bourn
  No traveler returns, puzzles the will…"
  (3.1.84–88).

This famous speech has Hamlet contemplating the mysteries of death. The subject is not simple, and neither is the poetry. Instead of rhyme, Hamlet uses assonance, matching vowel sounds with varying consonants.

- *Julius Caesar*, "And, thus un<u>braced</u>, Casca, as you <u>see</u>,
  Have <u>bared</u> my bosom to the thunder-<u>stone</u>;
  And when the cross blue lightning <u>seemed</u> to <u>open</u>…" (1.3.51–53).

This speech by Cassius contains a number of examples of assonance, including examples within the lines of poetry and at the end of the lines. The words "stone" and "open" are a particularly good example. The accented vowel sound is the same, but "open" has an additional syllable at the end of the word. Likewise, "unbraced" and "bared" share the same accented vowel sound, but their concluding consonants are different. In this way, Cassius avoids the excess formality of rhyme while maintaining eloquence in his rhetoric.

Asyndeton

- *Hamlet*, "Thus was I, sleeping, by a brother's hand
  <u>Of life, of crown, of queen</u>, at once dispatched,
  Cut off, even in the blossoms of my sin,
  <u>Unhouseled, disappointed, unaneled</u>,
  No reck'ning made, but sent to my account
  With all my imperfections on my head"
  (1.5.81–86).

Twice in this passage, the Ghost omits the coordinating conjunctions in a list of items: once in the objects of a preposition and once in a set of past participles forming passive verbs. He was dispatched "of life, of crown, of queen" and he was "unhouseled, disappointed, unaneled" by his brother. The lists of his woes—what has been robbed from him and what has been done to him—are incomplete; he could continue to add to both lists indefinitely.

- *Macbeth*, "But I have none. The king-becoming graces,
  <u>As justice, verity, temp'rance, stableness,</u>
  <u>Bounty, perseverance, mercy, lowliness,</u>
  <u>Devotion, patience, courage, fortitude,</u>
  I have no relish of them, but abound
  In the division of each several crime,
  Acting it many ways…" (4.3.107–113).

From his refuge in England, Malcolm pretends to be a scoundrel in order to test Macduff's dedication to the throne of Scotland. Adding to his ploy, as he names the qualities of a king that he claims not to have, he leaves the list unfinished, suggesting that a true king possesses more virtues than he has time or will to name.

Chiasmus

- *Henry V*, "<u>We</u> would not <u>die</u> in <u>that man's</u> company
   <u>That</u> fears his fellowship to <u>die</u> with <u>us</u>"
   (4.3.38–39).

In his speech before the battle of Agincourt, King Henry stirs up the flagging spirits of his men to fight. This is another example of his rhetorical prowess. Instead of telling the frightened men that they must stay, he rather encourages them to go, saying that he does not want to share the coming day's glory with any man who prefers not to participate. This example of chiasmus states his argument concisely: we do not want to die with any man if that man does not want to die with us. The verb stays the same, but the subject and object change places from one half of the line to the other so that the cowardly man is bookended by the plural pronoun referencing the brave soldiers Henry goes on to call "We few, we happy few, we band of brothers."

- *Macbeth*, "<u>Fair is foul, and foul is fair</u>.
   Hover through the fog and filthy air" (1.1.12–13).

Foreshadowing the way the kingdom of Scotland will be overturned during the course of the play, the witches describe the opening state of affairs using chiasmus. Fair things are now foul, and things once foul are now fair.

Consonance

- *Hamlet*, "The single and peculiar life is <u>bound</u>
   With all the strength and armor of the <u>mind</u>
   To keep itself from noyance, but much more
   That spirit upon whose weal depends and rests
   The lives of many…" (3.3.12–16).

You may notice that some characters in the play speak in poetry or verse while others speak in prose. Often, Shakespeare used these two ways of speaking to distinguish the nobility from the commoners and formal speech from casual exchanges. Some characters, like Hamlet, easily transition between the two. When characters speak in verse, rather than using full rhyme, they may use consonance, which adds beauty to the poetry without trapping the poet with the obligation to find exact rhymes.

- *Macbeth*, "Art not without ambition, but without
   The illness should attend it. What thou wouldst <u>highly</u>,
   That wouldst thou <u>holily</u>…" (1.5.19–22).

As Lady Macbeth muses about her husband's supposed weakness of character, she demonstrates her power as a rhetorician. The two terms she links using consonance—"highly" and "holily"—sound very similar, but their meanings are distinct. High things—in other words, those that are royal in nature or power-driven—are often incompatible with holy behavior.

Epistrophe

- *Hamlet*, "If thou hast any sound or use of voice,
   <u>Speak to me</u>.
   If there be any good thing to be done
   That may to thee do ease and grace to me,
   <u>Speak to me</u>.
   If thou art privy to thy country's fate,
   Which, happily, foreknowing may avoid,
   <u>Oh, speak</u>!" (1.1.140–147).

As Horatio entreats the Ghost to speak, he closes each request with some variation of the phrase "speak to me." Whatever else he asks the Ghost to do, his most desperate need is to hear the Ghost say something.

- *Julius Caesar*, "Who is here so base that would be a bondman? <u>If any, speak, for him have I offended</u>. Who is here so rude
   that would not be a Roman? <u>If any, speak, for him have I offended</u>. Who is here so vile that will not love
   his country? <u>If any, speak; for him have I offended</u>. I pause for a reply" (3.2.30–36).

Brutus gives the mob multiple opportunities to condemn him for the murder of Caesar; however, he phrases each offer in such a way that to protest would be to declare oneself a bondman, not a Roman, and a vile man who hates his country. According to Brutus's logic, the only people offended by Caesar's death are these types of people.

- *Julius Caesar*, "Come I to speak in Caesar's funeral.
   He was my friend, faithful and just to me;
   <u>But Brutus says he was ambitious;</u>
   <u>And Brutus is an honorable man.</u>
   He hath brought many captives home to Rome,
   Whose ransoms did the general coffers fill.

Examples from Challenge III Literature

Did this in Caesar seem ambitious?
When that the poor have cried, Caesar hath wept;
Ambition should be made of sterner stuff.
<u>Yet Brutus says he was ambitious,</u>
<u>And Brutus is an honorable man</u>" (3.2.93–103).

When Antony begins to speak in Caesar's defense, he uses the same technique that Brutus used: epistrophe. On the surface, he confirms Brutus's assertion that Caesar was ambitious; however, the prologue to each of those refrains is evidence against Caesar's ambitious nature. Those listening begin to hear the sarcasm in Antony's words, and they begin to question the idea that Brutus is honorable.

Foreshadowing

- *Romeo and Juliet*, "<u>My life were better ended by their hate</u>,
  Than death prorogued, wanting of thy love" (act 2, scene 2).

Shakespeare's play consistently points toward Romeo and Juliet's tragic end. Passages like this one foreshadow the choices that the young lovers will eventually make.

- *Julius Caesar*, "Run to your houses, fall upon your knees,
  Pray to the gods to intermit <u>the plague</u>
  <u>That needs must light on this ingratitude</u>" (act 1, scene 1).

This speech, one of the first in the play, creates an immediate sense of unease for the audience. Something is out of balance; something is not right, and theatergoers are now waiting to see if and how the plague that Marullus predicts will appear.

Hyperbole

- *Julius Caesar*, "And when you saw his chariot but appear,
  Have you not made an universal shout,
  <u>That Tiber trembled underneath her banks</u>
  To hear the replication of your sounds
  Made in her concave shores?" (1.1.48–52).

Marullus knows that the Tiber River did not literally shake when the people shouted at Pompey's approach. He uses hyperbole to remind the commoners how devoted they were to Pompey and to express his disgust that now they cheer equally loudly for Pompey's conqueror.

- *Macbeth*, "What hands are here? Ha! They pluck out mine eyes.
  Will all great Neptune's ocean wash this blood
  Clean from my hand? <u>No, this my hand will rather</u>
  <u>The multitudinous seas incarnadine,</u>
  <u>Making the green one red</u>" (2.2.77–81).

Macbeth's hand is not bloody enough to turn the oceans of the world from green to red, but in his sense of guilt, he imagines that his hands will never be clean again, using hyperbole to express this sentiment.

Imagery

- *Julius Caesar*, "<u>And yesterday the bird of night did sit</u>
  <u>Even at noonday upon the market-place,</u>
  <u>Hooting and shrieking</u>. When these prodigies
  Do so conjointly meet, let not men say,
  'These are their reasons, they are natural,'
  For I believe they are portentous things
  Unto the climate that they point upon"
  (1.3.26–32).

Describing the climate of Rome under Caesar's rule, Casca uses vivid natural imagery to indicate how unbalanced the world has become. As long as Caesar is in control, even night creatures like the owl make an appearance in the full noontime sun.

- *Macbeth*, "<u>And Duncan's horses (a thing most strange and certain)</u>,
  Beauteous and swift, the minions of their race,
  <u>Turned wild in nature, broke their stalls, flung out,</u>
  <u>Contending 'gainst obedience, as they would</u>
  <u>make war with mankind</u>…" (2.4.17–22).

After Duncan's death, those loyal to him notice the chaos into which Scotland has been flung. Ross describes the upheaval in Duncan's stables, using this imagery of broken stall doors to suggest that even the animals sense a disturbance brought on by the king's death.

Litotes

- *Macbeth*, "We will establish our estate upon
  Our eldest, Malcolm, whom we name hereafter
  The Prince of Cumberland; which honor must
  <u>Not unaccompanied</u> invest him only,

But signs of nobleness, like stars, shall shine
On all deservers…" (1.4.43–48).

In conferring his estate upon his son Malcolm, Duncan reminds his listeners that Malcolm is not the only one being rewarded on this day. Others will also receive "signs of nobleness." He uses a double negative to head off any complaints that he has not treated the other nobles justly or been unappreciative of their efforts on his behalf.

- *Julius Caesar*, "CASSIUS: Antony,
    The posture of your blows are yet unknown,
    But for your words, they rob the Hybla bees,
    And leave them honeyless.

    ANTONY: Not stingless too" (5.1.34–38).

Hybla was a town on the slopes of Mount Etna in Sicily that was renowned for its honey. Cassius means his statement as an insult, saying that Antony's words are like a sneak thief capable of stealing honey without being stung by the bees. Antony turns the metaphor around to suggest that his words strike home. He uses Cassius's same construction ("honeyless" / "stingless") but through a double negative is able to infer that his words in fact do have a sting and are dangerous to Cassius.

Metaphor

- *Much Ado About Nothing*, "When you went onward
    on this ended action,
    I looked upon her with a soldier's eye,
    That liked, but had a rougher task in hand
    Than to drive liking to the name of love.
    But now I am returned and that war thoughts
    Have left their places vacant, in their rooms
    Come thronging soft and delicate desires,
    All prompting me how fair young Hero is,
    Saying I liked her ere I went to wars"
    (1.1.292–300).

Claudio describes his mind and memory as a house, a common metaphor in Renaissance poetry. When one set of thoughts, those about war, leave the house, they make room for another set of thoughts, those about love.

- *Henry V*, "When we have matched our rackets to
    these balls,
    We will in France, by God's grace, play a set
    Shall strike his father's crown into the hazard"
    (1.2.272–274).

The crown prince of France, the Dauphin, insults Henry by sending him a set of tennis balls in response to his claim that part of France is his by right. In response, Henry uses a tennis metaphor to describe what he will do to the French kingdom. The metaphor speaks of the French crown (itself a metonym for the king's rule) as a tennis ball and represents battle as a tennis match.

Metonymy

- *Julius Caesar*, "…With this I depart: that, as I
    slew my best lover for the good of Rome, I have
    the same dagger for myself when it shall please my
    country to need my death" (3.2.46–49).

Having slain Caesar, Brutus promises that if he ever becomes a tyrant like Caesar, he will accept the same death. His reference is twofold, including both the physical dagger with which he stabbed Caesar and also the more abstract tyrant's death, for the good of the nation, which he claims Caesar received.

- *Macbeth*, "That, trusted home,
    Might yet enkindle you unto the crown,
    Besides the Thane of Cawdor" (1.3.132–134).

Banquo warns Macbeth against placing too much stock in the witches' prophecies. If he trusts them, Banquo says, he might be inspired to seek the kingship. He uses the closely associated object, the crown, to stand in for the authority and power of the king.

Onomatopoeia

- *Macbeth*, "A sailor's wife had chestnuts in her lap
    And munched, and munched, and munched…"
    (1.3.4–5).

The word "munch" replicates the sound caused by chewing crunchy items like chestnuts, while repetition of the word mimics the rhythm of chewing. The First Witch's playful and poetic speech helps listeners hear the sound effects of the story she tells.

- *Julius Caesar*, "The exhalations, whizzing in the air,
    Give so much light that I may read by them"
    (2.1.46–47).

Brutus describes the sound of lightning using a word that imitates the sound of rapid movement through the air. The "z" sound in particular catches the listener's ear and adds color to Brutus's imagery.

Parallelism

- *Hamlet*, "Give every man thy ear, but few thy voice.
    Take each man's censure, but reserve thy
    judgment.
    Costly thy habit as thy purse can buy,
    But not expressed in fancy (rich, not gaudy),
    For the apparel oft proclaims the man,
    And they in France of the best rank and station
    Are of a most select and generous chief in that"
    (1.3.74–80).

Parallelism permits a poet to condense his speech by eliminating sentence elements that would otherwise be repeated. Speaking in full sentences, Polonius might say, "Give every man thy ear, but give few men thy voice"; however, the parallel structure of the clauses allows him to eliminate the second "give" and "men" without confusing his listeners.

- *Julius Caesar*, "…As Caesar loved me, I weep for him. As he was fortunate, I rejoice at it. As he was valiant, I honor him. But, as he was ambitious, I slew him. There is tears for his love, joy for his fortune, honor for his valor, and death for his ambition" (3.2.26–30).

Brutus uses parallel clauses to justify his behavior toward Caesar. Each dependent clause is structured using "as" (meaning loosely "in that" or "because") plus one of Caesar's qualities; each independent clause begins with "I" plus one of Brutus's responses. Using this structure, Brutus shows the Romans how his view of Caesar—and his resulting actions—changed over time.

Personification

- *Much Ado About Nothing*, "Is it possible disdain
    should die while she hath such meet
    food to feed it as Signior Benedick? Courtesy
    itself must convert to disdain, if you come in her
    presence" (1.1.118–121).

In the previous line, Benedick refers to Beatrice as "Lady Disdain." In this passage, Beatrice carries through the device, speaking of both disdain and courtesy as though they were human.

- *Henry V*, "For now sits Expectation in the air
    And hides a sword, from hilts unto the point,
    With crowns imperial, crowns and coronets
    Promised to Harry and his followers" (2.0.8–11).

The Chorus describes for the theatergoers the state of mind among King Henry's followers at Southampton. They are excited by the expectation that they will be victorious. To express this mood more vividly, the Chorus personifies Expectation as an onlooker or a god.

Polysyndeton

- *Henry V*, "A noble shalt thou have, and present pay,
    And liquor likewise will I give to thee,
    And friendship shall combine, and brotherhood"
    (2.1.105–107).

Pistol promises Nym that if they forestall their duel, he will pay him a noble (six shillings eight pence) immediately and give him liquor and friendship. The use of polysyndeton demonstrates that Pistol is bargaining, adding offer to offer in a perennially incomplete list until Nym agrees.

- *Macbeth*, "…Alas, poor country,
    Almost afraid to know itself. It cannot
    Be called our mother, but our grave, where nothing
    But who knows nothing, is once seen to smile;
    Where sighs and groans and shrieks that rent the air
    Are made, not marked; where violent sorrow seems
    A modern ecstasy…" (4.3.189–195).

When Ross tells Malcolm about the state of Scotland, he uses polysyndeton to indicate the depth of his grief and the turmoil of the country, which goes on and on without an identifiable end.

Rhyme

- *Much Ado About Nothing*, "Where honeysuckles
    ripened by the sun,
    Forbid the sun to enter, like favorites
    Made proud by princes, that advance their pride
    Against that power that bred it. There will she hide her
    To listen our purpose. This is thy office"
    (3.1.8–13).

Rhyme does not have to occur in the final words of a line. As in this example, rhyme may include an unaccented syllable ("her") after the accented (stressed) rhyming syllable ("hide").

- *Hamlet*, "…The spirit that I have seen
   May be a devil, and the devil hath power
   T'assume a pleasing shape; yea, and perhaps,
   Out of my weakness and my melancholy,
   As he is very potent with such spirits,
   Abuses me to damn me. I'll have grounds
   More relative than this. <u>The play's the thing</u>
   Wherein I'll catch the <u>conscience of the King</u>"
   (2.2.627–634).

Blank verse was the dominant form used in Shakespeare's plays and those of his contemporaries. Blank verse refers to poetry written without a regular rhyme scheme but with a specific meter, called iambic pentameter. Typically, each line has five stressed or accented syllables in a pattern of unstressed–stressed. Although blank verse does not consistently rhyme, as a cue to the audience that an act or scene was at an end, many scenes conclude with a rhymed couplet, or two rhyming lines at the end of a speech, like the one in the above example.

Simile

- *Hamlet*, "Thy knotted and combined locks to part,
   And each particular hair to stand on end
   <u>Like quills upon the fretful porcupine</u>"
   (1.5.24–26).

The Ghost builds anticipation for the news he will deliver to Hamlet by foretelling its effect on the hearer. Hamlet's hair, he predicts, will stand on end like the quills of a porcupine. This simile is additionally significant because according to early modern animal lore, the porcupine could detach its quills at will and shoot them at its enemies. In a sense, the Ghost is saying that once he tells his story, Hamlet will transform from a harmless creature to one that is armed and ready to attack.

- *Julius Caesar*, "Now could I, Casca, name to thee a man
   Most <u>like this dreadful night,</u>
   That thunders, lightens, opens graves, and roars
   <u>As doth the lion</u> in the Capitol;
   A man no mightier than thyself or me
   In personal action, yet prodigious grown,
   And fearful, as these strange eruptions are"
   (1.3.75–81).

Similes can be a persuasive tool, as in this speech by Cassius. Indirect, metaphorical speech fuels the emotions while shielding the speaker from persecution. When Cassius paints word pictures for Casca rather than naming Caesar outright, he protects himself: if Casca attempts to turn on him, he can claim that Casca mistook his meaning.

Synecdoche

- *Much Ado About Nothing*, "BENEDICK: To bind me or undo me—one of them.
   Signior Leonato, truth it is, good signior,
   Your niece regards me with <u>an eye of favor</u>.
   LEONATO: <u>That eye my daughter lent her</u>; 'tis most true.
   BENEDICK: And I do with an eye of love requite her" (5.4.20–24).

Benedick acknowledges that Beatrice loves him, but to do so, he speaks of her "eye of favor." The listener understands that he is referring to Beatrice using the part of her body associated with the ability to see someone and fall in love, the eye.

- *Henry V*, "And, to relief of lazars and weak age
   Of <u>indigent faint souls</u> past corporal toil"
   (1.1.15–16).

Canterbury laments the funds that would be lost to the Church if the king approved a measure proposed by the commoners. As he explains what the sum would otherwise buy, he speaks of giving aid to the elderly and infirm who can no longer do physical labor. Instead of speaking of the elderly themselves, he refers instead to souls, using them to stand in for the people to whom they belong.

For Further Reading

Harmon, William, and Hugh Holman. *A Handbook to Literature*. 10th ed. Upper Saddle River, NJ: Pearson/Prentice Hall, 2006.

Kern, Andrew. *The Lost Tools of Writing: Level 1*. 4th ed. Concord, NC: The CiRCE Institute, 2011.

Leithart, Peter J. *Brightest Heaven of Invention: A Christian Guide to Six Shakespeare Plays*. Moscow, ID: Canon Press, 1996.

Rhodes, Suzanne. *The Roar on the Other Side: A Guide for Student Poets*. Moscow, ID: Canon Press, 2000.

Richards, I. A. *The Philosophy of Rhetoric*. New York: Oxford UP, 1936.

Bibliography

Shakespeare, William. *Much Ado About Nothing*. Ed. Barbara A. Mowat and Paul Werstine. New York: Simon & Schuster, 2009. Print.

———. *Romeo and Juliet*. Ed. Barbara A. Mowat and Paul Werstine. New York: Simon & Schuster. 2004. Print.

———.*The Life of Henry V*. Ed. Barbara A. Mowat and Paul Werstine. New York: Simon & Schuster, 2009. Print.

———.*The Tragedy of Hamlet, Prince of Denmark*. Ed. Barbara A. Mowat and Paul Werstine. New York: Simon & Schuster, 2012. Print.

———.*The Tragedy of Julius Caesar*. Ed. Barbara A. Mowat and Paul Werstine. New York: Simon & Schuster, 2011. Print.

———.*The Tragedy of Macbeth*. Ed. Barbara A. Mowat and Paul Werstine. New York: Simon & Schuster, 2013. Print.

EXAMPLES FROM

Challenge IV

LITERATURE

Examples from Challenge IV Literature

Early Greek epic poetry was the product of an oral culture that relied on storytelling for its mythology and history. Storytellers used formulas, repetition, and sounds that were pleasing to the ear in order to stir the memories of their listeners and also to aid the reciter. Homer is the most famous of the ancient Greek bards. His *Iliad* and *Odyssey* are thought to be loosely historical, describing events in the twelfth century BC, but Homer likely composed them around the eighth century BC. Later Greek authors like Hesiod and Sophocles further developed Homer's themes of fate and heroism while refining the Greek language for their own purposes.

Some of the greatest Roman works, including Virgil's *Aeneid* (c. 29–19 BC), were written under a patronage system similar to that of Renaissance England. Although the Romans took inspiration from the culture and literature of the Greeks they conquered, their writing was more terse and precise, emphasizing the glory of the nation over the heroism of the individual. Latin works use many traditional Greek rhetorical devices that translate well into English, including alliteration, parallelism, asyndeton, and anaphora. However, Latin is also a highly inflected language (i.e., word endings, rather than sentence position, designate parts of speech). That means Latin is well suited for the use of hyperbaton, the rearrangement of words in a sentence to create a particular effect.

Every language is intertwined with the culture of the people who speak it. For example, Latin uses many war-related metaphors and has multiple words for "wound" and "fight" because the Roman Empire was a military society. Some of the nuances of language get lost or muted in translation—all the more reason to study multiple languages, both ancient and modern! Nonetheless, we can still gain a sense of the beauty in ancient languages by studying them in translation. All of these works are available in multiple editions and translations, so unless you are using the same edition as the one cited in the bibliography, line numbers may not match precisely, and translations may vary slightly. Reading a passage in multiple translations may give you an even richer understanding of the material.

Alliteration

- *The Aeneid*, "…multosque per annos errabant, acti fatis, maria omnia circum. Tantae molis erat Romanam condere gentem!"

  "…For years,
  They wandered as their <u>destiny</u> <u>drove</u> them on
  From one sea to the next: so <u>hard</u> and <u>huge</u>
  A task it was to found the Roman people" (p. 4, lines 46–49).

This is an example of the differences between Latin and English poetry. In this passage, the translator uses alliteration of the sounds "d" and "h" to add beauty to the struggle endured by the Trojan exiles. As you can see, the alliteration is not present in the Latin.

- *The Aeneid*, "Because of one man's one mad act—the crime
  Of Ajax, son of Oïleus? She—yes, she!—
  Hurled out of <u>cloudland lancing</u> fire of Jove" (p. 5, lines 62–64).

This example from *The Aeneid* demonstrates alliteration on both the letter "l" and the syllable "an." When recited aloud, it requires precise enunciation and draws attention to the shift from the rounded "l" sounds to the sharp "f" sound of the next word, "fire."

- *Oedipus Rex*, "Not <u>so</u> to <u>say</u> for <u>c</u>ertain; <u>s</u>peak again" (p. 14).

Oedipus's words to Tiresias rely heavily on alliteration with the "s" sound, creating an effect like the hissing of a snake or a human whisper. It is an eerie sound, enhancing the growing unease that Oedipus feels as he uncovers the mystery of his father's death.

Allusion

- *Oedipus Rex*, "Whose coming to our Cadmean town released
  The toll we paid, of <u>a hard Sorceress</u>,
  And that, without instruction or advice
  Of our imparting; but of Heaven it came" (p. 2).

According to a footnote in the text, the Priest alludes to the Sphinx, whose riddle Oedipus had guessed, thus freeing the land of Thebes from her curse. In doing so, Oedipus had won the kingship of Thebes and the hand of the queen in marriage.

- *The Odyssey*, "In came the herald now,
  leading along the faithful bard the Muse adored
  above all others, true, but her gifts were mixed
  with good and evil both: <u>she stripped him of sight</u>
  but gave the man the power of stirring, rapturous
  song" (p. 193, 8.71–76).

Some allusions are more certain than others. Many early students and critics of Homer took this passage to be an allusion to Homer himself, who was rumored to be blind. Present-day scholars can gather evidence for one side or the other, but they cannot—as of yet—prove that Homer was or was not blind. The difficulty of studying ancient literature is that many of the **referents** (the events, places, or figures to which allusions refer) are difficult to determine or verify.

Anaphora

- *Theogony*, "…From there they go forth, veiled in thick
  mist, and walk by night, uttering beautiful voice, singing
  of Zeus who bears the aegis,
  <u>and</u> the lady Hera of Argos, who walks in sandals of gold,
  <u>and</u> the daughter of Zeus the aegis-bearer, pale-eyed Athene,
  <u>and</u> Phoebus Apollo, and Artemis the archer,
  <u>and</u> Poseidon earth-charioted, shaker of the earth,
  <u>and</u> holy Themis, and Aphrodite of curling lashes,
  <u>and</u> Hebe of gold diadem, <u>and</u> fair Dione,
  Leto, Iapetos, and crooked-schemer Kronos…" (p. 1).

Listing the gods, Hesiod uses anaphora to place emphasis on each of the principal gods he names. The repetition lends force to the list of names, and the simultaneous use of polysyndeton leads the reader to recognize that each one is a powerful being in his or her own right.

- *The Odyssey*, "Telemachus asked his loyal
  serving-man at last,
  'Old friend, <u>where does</u> this stranger come from?
  <u>Why did</u> the sailors land him here in Ithaca?
  <u>Who did</u> they say they are?
  I hardly think he came this way on foot'" (p. 340, 16.63–67).

Characteristic of *The Odyssey*, and Greek epic poetry more broadly, is the ritual of introduction. Additional examples can be found in Book 15, lines 293–294, and in Book 7, lines 272–276. The stock set of questions—typically including identity, place of origin, and parentage—gives the poet a convenient reason to narrate events that took place "off-stage." This convention also gives present-day readers insight into the cultural values of the ancient Greeks. Parentage and clan affiliation played a central role in determining how a stranger should be received and if he could be trusted. Other examples of introduction rites in *The Odyssey* lump all of the questions together, but here, by starting each line with a separate question, the translator extends the moment of anticipation for the father-son reunion that will take place less than two hundred lines later.

Antithesis

- *Oedipus Rex*, "And since you have reproached me with my blindness,
  I say—<u>you have your sight and do not see</u>
  What evils are about you, nor with whom,
  Nor in what home you are dwelling…" (p. 15).

As Tiresias speaks to the senator and Oedipus, he seems to contradict himself, saying that Oedipus can see and yet cannot see. His use of antithesis actually reveals a deeper truth in the play by contrasting two different meanings of the word "sight." Oedipus can use his ocular senses, and yet he is blind to the truth about his destiny. This statement also foreshadows Oedipus's self-imposed punishment at the end of the play, when the king's figurative inability to see will influence his physical ability to see.

- *The Odyssey*, "And I saw Leda next, Tyndareus' wife,
    who'd borne the king two sons, intrepid twins,
    Castor, breaker of horses, and the hardy boxer Polydeuces,
    <u>both buried now in the life-giving earth though still alive</u>.
    Even under the earth Zeus grants them that distinction:
    <u>one day alive, the next day dead</u>, each twin by turns,
    they both hold honors equal to the gods'" (p. 259, 11.341–347).

In Latin, Castor and Polydeuces (Pollux) are known as *Gemini* (the Twins), and they are the namesakes of the constellation. According to Greek and Roman mythology, Castor is the son of the mortal king Tyndareus, while Polydeuces is the immortal son of Zeus. When Castor is killed, Polydeuces petitions to share his immortality with his twin. As a result, they take turns living with the gods and lying dead under the ground. According to other accounts, they are given an alternate immortality among the stars. The poet uses antithesis to explain this complex story through the seeming contradiction of being dead and alive at the same time.

Apostrophe

- *The Iliad*, "Anger be now your song, <u>immortal one</u>,
    Akhilleus' anger, doomed and ruinous,
    that caused the Akhaians loss on bitter loss…" (p. 5, 1.1–3).

Homer invokes the Muses at the start of his poem to provide inspiration and wisdom to his poetic endeavor. In classical mythology, the Muses were the goddesses that embodied knowledge and inspired creators of literature, science, and the arts. Alternately numbered as three or nine, they were the daughters of Zeus and Mnemosyne (memory).

- *The Aeneid*, "Tell me the causes now, <u>O Muse</u>, how galled
    In her divine pride, and how sore at heart
    From her old wound, the queen of gods compelled him—
    A man apart, devoted to his mission—" (p. 3, lines 13–16).

Like Homer, Virgil invokes the Muses at the start of his poem, but unlike Homer, he names them explicitly.

Assonance

- *The Iliad*, "'…Hêra's pleading
    <u>swayed</u> them all, and bitter days from Zeus
    <u>await</u> the Trojans.' Hold on to this message
    against forgetfulness in tides of day
    when blissful sleep is gone" (p. 20, 2.36–40).

Two lines in this passage demonstrate assonance with the long "a" sound, but the device is present at the beginning rather than the end of the line. Because Homer's poetry was delivered orally, devices like this would attract the listeners' attention and make the poetry flow smoothly into their ears.

- *The Odyssey*, "Many cities of men he saw and learned their minds,
    many pains he suffered, heartsick on the open sea,
    fighting to save his life and bring his comrades <u>home</u>.
    But he could not save them from disaster, hard as he <u>strove</u>—" (p. 77, 1.4–7).

The long "o" sound in the two final lines is the same, but the final consonants differ, preventing this from being an example of true rhyme. Even when a poet does not strive for rhyme, his or her efforts to create fluid verse that is pleasing to the ear may produce this type of near rhyme. This passage also features anaphora, as the first two clauses contain the same opening word and the same sentence structure.

- *The Odyssey*, "But now I must go back to my <u>swift trim ship</u>
    and all my shipmates, chafing there, I'm sure,
    waiting for my return. It all rests with you" (p. 87, 1.348–350).

Speaking to Telemachus, Athena emphasizes her need for haste with three consecutive words containing the same short "i" sound. This type of assonance requires precise enunciation from the speaker and is designed to grab listeners' attention.

Asyndeton

- *The Iliad*, "…And Kalkhas,
    Kalkhas Thestórides, came forward, wisest
    by far of all who scanned the flight of birds.

He knew what was, what had been, what would be,
Kalkhas, who brought Akhaia's ships to Ilion
by the diviner's gift Apollo gave him" (pp. 7–8, 1.79–84).

This passage uses asyndeton, leaving out the final coordinating conjunction that grammar would demand, to meet the metrical requirements of the line (five stressed syllables being typical of blank verse). An additional effect is to show that for the diviner Kalkhas, the past, present, and future are all equally accessible realms of knowledge.

- *The Iliad*, "'Don't be a fool!
   It isn't like you to desert the field
   the way some coward would! Come, halt, command
   the troops back to their seats. You don't yet know what Agamémnon means'" (p. 35, 2.216–220).

Asyndeton can be used to issue commands or to connote a commanding attitude. This use is common in Latin, as in Caesar's famous statement, "*Veni, vidi, vici*" ("I came, I saw, I conquered.") It is also present in this rallying cry from Odysseus to the deserting Greeks.

Chiasmus

- *Theogony*, "…every man is fortunate whom the Muses love; the
   voice flows sweet from his lips…" (p. 6, lines 96–97).

This example shows the way chiasmus can appear on a micro level, in individual words, as well as on the macro level of clauses or sentences. The two underlined words run together because the final two letters of "flows" are the same, but reversed, in the word "sweet." Readers of poetry are better equipped to see this feature, but listeners might still notice the smooth quality of the language.

- *Oedipus Rex*, "And hearken and receive my words, which I—
   A stranger to this tale, and to the deed
   A stranger—shall pronounce; for of myself
   I could not follow up the traces far…" (p. 9, III.2.17–20).

This passage demonstrates anaphora as well as chiasmus. Oedipus renames himself in two ways.

The phrase is reordered in a chiasmus to place "a stranger" at the beginning and end of the phrase. This translation deliberately uses enjambment so that two consecutive lines begin with "a stranger," emphasizing Oedipus's anxious need to place himself outside the events plaguing Thebes.

Consonance

- *The Iliad*, "'The gods who hold Olympos, may they grant you
   plunder of Priam's town and a fair wind home,
   but let me have my daughter back for ransom
   as you revere Apollo, son of Zeus!'" (p. 5, 1.23–26).

Both of these lines conclude with a similar consonantal sound, "m," but the pronunciation of the preceding vowel differs. This is characteristic of Fitzgerald's translation, which prefers loose blank verse to rhymed verse, claiming it comes closer to Homer's Greek hexameter (approximately six stressed syllables per line).

- *The Odyssey*, "…and wipe all thought of Ithaca from his mind.
   But he, straining for no more than a glimpse
   of hearth-smoke drifting up from his own land,
   Odysseus longs to die…" (p. 79, 1.68–71).

As Athena describes Odysseus's plot to Zeus, this translation uses emphatic language and repeated consonant sounds to drive her point home. In this example, "mind" and land" share the same concluding consonant sound, but the preceding vowel differs.

Epistrophe

- *The Iliad*, "…he too attacked but failed to break the Danääns,
   whose line of shields made them a barrier,
   spearpoints advanced, compact around Patróklos.
   ……………………………………………..
   And safe, you'd say, was neither sun nor moon,
   since all was darkened in the battle-cloud—
   as were the champions who held and fought
   around the dead Patróklos" (pp. 412–413; 17.398–400, 412–415).

After Hektor kills Patróklos, an important phase of the battle revolves around possession of the young Greek's body. The rhetorical device of epistrophe, here demonstrated in the repeated closing line in two adjacent passages, is one way for an orator to direct his audience's attention to a central figure or issue.

- *The Odyssey*, "Only Antinous, who found it in himself to say,
  'So high and mighty, Telemachus—such unbridled rage!
  Well now, fling your accusations <u>at *us*</u>?
  Think to pin the blame <u>on *us*</u>? You think again'" (p. 96, 2.90–93).

Antinous is furious that Telemachus would hold him and the other suitors responsible for their pursuit of Penelope. He punctuates his indignation by concluding two subsequent lines with an emphatic "*us*?" implying that someone else is guilty of the misdeed.

Foreshadowing

- *The Iliad*, "Anger be now your song, immortal one, Akhilleus' anger, <u>doomed and ruinous</u>, <u>that caused the Akhaians loss on bitter loss</u> and crowded brave souls into the undergloom" (book 1, lines 1–4).

The opening lines of *The Iliad*, in true epic form, begin *in medias res* ("in the middle of things"). In them, we are told that Akhilleus' anger will be "doomed" and "ruinous." We learn that it will cause the Akhaians "loss on bitter loss." As a result, the reader's mind is already full of questions: Why is Akhilleus angry? What will happen as a result? Homer's use of foreshadowing captures the reader's attention and holds it.

- *The Odyssey*, "He snatched a winged arrow lying bare on the board—
  the rest still bristled deep inside the quiver,
  <u>soon to be tasted by all the feasters there</u>" (book 21, lines 463–465).

As a disguised Odysseus sets out to beat his wife's suitors in an archery contest, Homer takes this opportunity to foreshadow Odysseus' revenge: the rest of the arrows are "soon to be tasted by all the feasters there."

Hyperbole

- *The Odyssey*, "But now this...
  a worse disaster that soon will <u>grind my house down</u>,
  ruin it all, and all my worldly goods in the bargain" (pp. 94–95, 2.51–53).

Telemachus's dire predictions are made more potent by the use of literary exaggeration. The suitors are not literally using stones to grind his house to the ground; rather, in this combination of hyperbole and metonymy, their greediness is depleting the family's resources and damaging their reputation.

- *The Aeneid*, "Like blood-stained Mars himself he rode, when Mars
  Goes headlong by the frozen Hebrus river,
  Beating out claps of thunder on his shield
  And lashing on his furious team for war—
  That team <u>that on the open ground outruns</u>
  <u>The south and west winds</u>, while the farthest land
  Of Thrace re-echoes to their drumming hooves" (pp. 379–380, lines 454–460).

In Greek and Roman mythology, the gods are defined by hyperbole. They are superhuman, characterized by feats that would be impossible for a human to undertake. No mere team of horses could outrun the wind or be heard across the land of Thrace, a territory that extended from the Black Sea to the Aegean Sea, covering parts of present-day Greece, Macedonia, Bulgaria, and Turkey. The mythical horses of Mars, however, could do this. So, when Virgil describes the ride of Turnus as like that of Mars (a simile), he uses the god's features to amplify Turnus's speed and fury.

Imagery

- *The Iliad*, "Amid the ships and huts of the Myrmidons
  they found him, taking joy in <u>a sweet harp</u>
  <u>of rich and delicate make—the crossbar set</u>
  <u>to hold the strings being silver</u>. He had won it
  when he destroyed the city of Eëtíôn,
  and plucking it he took his joy: he sang
  old tales of heroes, while across the room
  alone and silent sat Patróklos, waiting
  until Akhilleus should be done with song" (p. 203, 9.223–231).

In this scene, Phoinix, Aías, and Odysseus go to Akhilleus in an effort to persuade him to return to the battle against the Trojans. The details with which Homer describes this scene may seem irrelevant, but they contain multiple layers of imagery. In Book 1, the Akhaians were forced to appease Apollo, who had been roused to wrath at Akhilleus's request. Now the Akhaians must appease Akhilleus, who sits playing a harp of Eëtíôn in the manner of Apollo (the invention of the harp was popularly credited to Apollo). Homer describes the harp in vivid detail, down to the silver crossbar.

- *The Odyssey*, "But then, <u>when the wheeling seasons brought the year around,
   that year spun out by the gods when he should reach his home,</u>
   Ithaca—though not even there would he be free of trials,
   even among his loved ones—then every god took pity,
   all except Poseidon" (p. 78, 1.19–23).

This passage vividly describes Homer's conception of the seasons and the phases of sun and moon. Scholars infer that Homer thought of the heavens as an inverted bowl, with the celestial bodies moving along its internal arc. This passage might also refer to a concept that would later become known as the *Rota Fortunae*, or Wheel of Fortune. Early descriptions of the wheel make it a three-dimensional globe on which a blind goddess stood, turning and changing the fate of men as it rolled. Later depictions make the orb more like a modern wheel, with Fortune as a capricious woman elevating one man and deposing another at whim.

- *The Odyssey*, "…And mother…
   she neither rejects a marriage she despises
   nor can she bear to bring the courting to an end—
   <u>while they continue to bleed my household white</u>"
   (p. 85, 1.289–292).

This passage contains a brilliant example of imagery. Most images revolving around blood use the color red and focus on the bloodstains left on the outside of the victim and anyone else present. In contrast, Telemachus describes the effect on a victim's skin, which is drained of color by the loss of blood, leaving the injured party—in this case Odysseus's household—an unhealthy white.

Litotes

- *Oedipus Rex*, "Fool, you reproach me as <u>not one of these
   Shall not reproach you</u>, soon!" (p. 14, III.2.190–191)

Oedipus scorns Tiresias's accusation, telling the seer that his ears, eyes, and mind are blind. In replying, Tiresias uses a double negative, instead of saying "all of these [ears, eyes, and mind] will reproach you." This technique adds sting to Tiresias's retort, and it also foreshadows Oedipus's loss of his eyes, which will not be able to reproach Tiresias after he stabs them.

- *The Odyssey*, "'How he leapt to his feet and off he went!
   No waiting around for proper introductions.
   And <u>no mean man</u>, not by the looks of him, I'd say'" (pp. 90–91, 1.467–469).

Eurymachus recognizes that there is something special about Telemachus's guest, the goddess Athena in disguise. Rather than saying simply that the "man" is wealthy or of good birth, he makes the same basic claim by negating the opposite, calling Athena "no mean man." This type of construction highlights the speaker's suspicion about the goddess's disguise.

Metaphor

- *The Aeneid*, "He said no more, but shut himself away
   And dropped <u>the reins of rule</u> over the state" (p. 217, lines 825–826).

As King Latinus loses sway over his kingdom, he withdraws from the fray. Virgil uses a metaphor to describe his abdication. Ruling a kingdom, he implies, is like riding a horse or driving a chariot. He does not make this comparison explicitly, as in a simile. Rather, he talks about ruling the kingdom in the same way that one would talk about riding a horse. If the rider gives up control, he might drop the reins, giving the horse its head. Similarly, Latinus drops the reins of the "horse" that is his kingdom.

- *Oedipus Rex*, "Well, if his bosom holds <u>a grain of fear</u>,
   Curses like yours he never will abide!" (p. 11, III.2.103–104).

In this passage, the Senator tells Oedipus that Tiresias must surely respond to his summons. He uses a metaphor to do so, implying that man's bosom is like a basket or other container full of grain. His emotions—fear, courage, or joy—are different types of grain. Just as one might have a basket full of wheat into which had slipped a few weeds, one might have a basket full of courage with a single grain of fear hidden at the bottom.

Metonymy

- *The Odyssey*, "'Still,' the clear-eyed goddess reassured him,
    'trust me, the gods have not marked out your house
    for such an unsung future,
    not if Penelope has borne a son like you'" (p. 84, 1.256–259).

The house in this passage does not refer to a wooden structure built by men. Rather, the word "house" is commonly used to stand in for the idea of a household—the people who inhabit the house—and, with it, the idea of a family line. Here, Athena uses metonymy to reassure Telemachus that his family line will not be without fame.

- *The Odyssey*, "'Well, Telemachus, only the gods could teach you
    to sound so high and mighty! Such brave talk.
    I pray that Zeus will never make *you* king of Ithaca,
    though your father's crown is no doubt yours by birth'" (p. 90, 1.441–444).

Metonymy is often used to talk about the institution of royalty. Objects have great symbolic meaning because they set the royal family apart from the general populace. Think about stories of kings, queens, princes, and princesses who go among the common people in disguise (Shakespeare's *Measure for Measure*, Twain's *The Prince and the Pauper*, or the fairy tale *Sleeping Beauty*). Without their crowns, robes, scepters, and thrones, they are not easy to distinguish. In this example, Antinous uses a related object, a crown, to refer to the kingship of Ithaca.

Onomatopoeia

- *The Odyssey*, "…He raged on, seething against the great Odysseus till he reached his native land" (p. 78, 1.23–24).

To form the word "seethe," the speaker must force air between his teeth, much as hot air or water would escape from a pot when it boils. The sound of the word thus mimics its meaning.

- *The Aeneid*, "At these words
    From Saturn's daughter, Allecto spread those wings
    That hiss with snakes and left the towering air
    For underworld again" (p. 216, lines 769–772).

The word "hiss," spoken, makes the same sound that a snake makes. Even though Virgil's poetry was written rather than oral, the long oral tradition of epic poetry caused readers to attend not only to the words but also to the sounds of the poem.

Parallelism

- *The Iliad*, "Honor the gods' will, they may honor ours" (p. 12, 1.256).

This sentence uses poetic devices on several levels. On the level of content, the sentence demonstrates a chiasmus. The "do unto others" ethic lends itself to a chiasmus: [Men] honor gods' will / gods honor men's will. On the level of structure, the sentence is parallel. The order of the two clauses is the same: [subject] + [verb] + [direct object].

- *The Odyssey*, "Something wounds me deeply…
    not news I've heard of an army on the march,
    word I've caught firsthand so I can warn you now,
    or some other public matter I'll disclose and argue.
    No, the crisis is my own" (p. 94, 2.44–48).

In this passage, Telemachus demonstrates his prowess as a budding orator. Because he speaks in a long, complicated sentence, he uses parallel form for each of the modifying phrases he adds to the structure. Each of these phrases builds the anticipation of his audience and drives their impatience to hear what crisis he means.

Personification

- *Theogony*, "Night bore hateful Doom and dark Fate and Death, she
    bore Sleep, she bore the tribe of Dreams" (p. 9, lines 211–212).

Many early Greek and Roman myths personify natural elements as gods and goddesses. Here, Hesiod portrays Night as a mother who gives birth to doom, fate, death, sleep, and dreams. The polytheistic worship of the Greeks derives from the same understanding of nature as controlled by the various gods who demand worship and sacrifice to appease their capricious tempers.

- ❦ *The Iliad*, "<u>When Dawn spread out her fingertips</u> of rose
  they put to sea for the main camp of Akhaians, and the Archer God sent them a following wind" (p. 21, 1.547–549).

In Greek myths, Dawn, also called Eos, is a female personification of the dawn, who brings new life to each day as the sun rises. Homer almost always refers to Dawn as rosy-fingered or having fingertips of rose. This pattern of naming a character using a familiar compound adjective is known as a "Homeric epithet."

- ❦ *The Aeneid*, "'Aeolus, the father
  Of gods and men decreed and fixed your power
  <u>To calm the waves or make them rise in wind</u>.
  The race I hate is crossing the Tuscan sea,
  Transporting Ilium with her household gods—
  Beaten as they are—to Italy" (p. 5, lines 91–96).

The image of calming waves or wind is such a common figure of speech that it may slip past your notice; however, it is an example of personification. Authors use this figure of speech when they want to suggest that the ocean or the winds are like a child or unruly animal that can be calmed by a human. In reality, waves are not subject to human mastery. For Jesus to rebuke the wind and have it respond (Mark 4), then, is even more miraculous.

Polysyndeton

- ❦ *Theogony*, "…they had the surname
  of Circle-eyes because of this one circular eye that lay on
  their forehead. <u>And strength and force and resource</u>
  were upon their works" (p. 7, lines 143–146).

This passage, describing the race of the Cyclopes, gives additional emphasis to the characteristics of these giants through the use of polysyndeton, separating the items in the list with coordinating conjunctions that are not grammatically necessary. Hesiod frequently employs this technique, and it is common in Greek and Roman writing. (Coordinating conjunctions in Latin are frequently doubled, including the suffix "–que" and the conjunction "et". The construction "et…et…" can be translated in several ways: "both…and," "as well as," and "not only…but also.")

- ❦ *Oedipus Rex*, "…Moreover all these things
  I charge you to accomplish, in behalf
  <u>Of me, and of the God, and of this land</u>,
  So ruined, barren and forsaken of Heaven" (p. 10, III.2.55–58).

When Oedipus tells the Cadmeans that they must reveal the person who was responsible for the death of the former king, Laius, he does not realize that he is speaking about himself. He charges them to turn in the murderer in his name, the god's name (Apollo), and the name of their cursed land. Notice the arrogance in the order he uses: Apollo is sandwiched between Oedipus and the land, and polysyndeton places all three on equal footing.

Rhyme

- ❦ *Oedipus Rex*, "O Prophecy of Jove, whose words are <u>sweet</u>,
  With what doom art thou <u>sent</u>
  To glorious Thebes, from Pytho's gilded <u>seat</u>?
  I am distraught with fearful <u>wonderment</u>…" (p. 6, I.1.1–4).

In Greek theater, the Chorus played a special role. Played by a group of actors, the Chorus mediated between the audience and the actors. Greek theaters were not intimate, and because of the size of the theater, actors' voices had to travel close to a hundred meters. The Chorus, wearing masks frozen in a particular expression, could convey more effectively a strong emotion than a single actor could. Their speeches often communicated directly with the audience, sharing wisdom and inviting the spectators to join in judging the actions of the protagonist. This translation of the Chorus rhymes ABAB. In other words, lines one and three rhyme ("sweet" and "seat") while lines two and four share a different rhyme ("sent" and "wonderment").

- ❦ *The Odyssey*, "And sparkling-eyed Athena drove the matter home:
  'Father, son of Cronus, our high and mighty <u>king</u>,
  surely he goes down to a death he earned in full!
  Let them all die so, all who do such <u>things</u>'" (p. 79, 1.53–56).

This is a rare instance of rhyme in Fagles's translation. It may be unintentional, or it may be intended to lend ornament to the speech of the goddess. In later plays of the Renaissance, verse forms, sometimes including rhyme, were used to distinguish the speech of noblemen from that of the commoners (prose). Others used rhyme to set apart a Chorus-like figure from those that do not directly speak to the audience.

Simile

- *The Iliad*, "From the camp
  the troops were turning out now, thick <u>as bees
  that issue from some crevice in a rock face,
  endlessly pouring forth, to make a cluster
  and swarm on blooms of summer here and there,
  glinting and droning, busy in bright air.</u>
  Like bees innumerable from ships and huts
  down the deep foreshore streamed those regiments
  toward the assembly ground…" (p. 32, 2.98–106).

The epic simile, a simile of extended length and intricacy, is characteristic of epic poetry like Homer's and Virgil's. This example begins with a simple comparison: "the troops were turning out now, thick as bees." Homer goes on to elaborate on the character, appearance, and behavior of the bees. A careless listener might almost forget the initial comparison and the true subject, the troops leaving the camp.

- *The Aeneid*, "Above the rest, Aeneas walked to meet her,
  To join his retinue with hers. He seemed—
  <u>Think of the lord Apollo in the spring
  When he leaves wintering in Lycia
  By Xanthus torrent, for his mother's isle
  Of Delos, to renew the festival;
  Around his altars Cretans, Dryopës,
  And painted Agathyrsans raise a shout,
  But the god walks the Cynthian ridge alone
  And smooths his hair, binds it in fronded laurel,
  Braids it in gold; and shafts ring on his shoulders.</u>
  So elated and swift, Aeneas walked
  With sunlit grace upon him" (pp. 100–101, lines 197–209).

This example is, at its most basic, a comparison between Aeneas and Apollo, who both walk swiftly, eagerly, and alone. The reader may not immediately understand that Aeneas is like Apollo, so Virgil goes into greater detail. The rest of the simile describes Apollo's manner when he visits his mother's island, which is like Aeneas's manner as he walks toward Dido. The reader is drawn into the simile itself, to the point that the original comparison is almost lost in the story of the one who is compared. Epic similes often connect a human hero to a greater mythological type from among the gods, showing humans to be part of a story greater than they.

Synecdoche

- *Oedipus Rex*, "Next, from <u>the bendings of thy golden string</u>
  I would see showered thy artillery
  Invincible, marshalled to succour me,
  Lycean King!" (p. 8, Chorus III.2.1–4).

The Chorus summons Apollo to bring judgment and restoration to Thebes. In this passage, the Chorus uses part of an object—"thy golden string"—to stand in for the whole—a bow and arrow, associated with Apollo. (In *The Iliad*, Apollo helps Paris shoot an arrow into the heel of Achilles.)

- *The Iliad*, "…I have seen more action
  <u>hand to hand</u> in those assaults than you have,
  but when the time for sharing comes, the greater
  share is always yours…" (p. 11, 1.192–195).

Hand-to-hand combat is a familiar image in English writing; however, read literally, this passage implies that the men's hands alone were involved in the combat. "Hand-to-hand" combat is a rhetorical device that uses the hand to stand in for the body as a whole. It signifies that the hands are the most important body part involved in the fighting and indicates that the fighting takes place at close range.

For Further Reading

Abbott, Frank Frost. *A Short History of Rome.* Chicago: Scott, Foresman, and Company, 1906.

Gardiner, Cynthia P. *The Sophoclean Chorus: A Study of Character and Function.* Iowa City: U. of Iowa, 1987.

Harmon, William, and Hugh Holman. *A Handbook to Literature.* 10th ed. Upper Saddle River, NJ: Pearson/Prentice Hall, 2006.

Highet, Gilbert. *Poets in a Landscape.* New York: Alfred A. Knopf, 1965.

Kern, Andrew. *The Lost Tools of Writing: Level 1.* 4th ed. Concord, NC: The CiRCE Institute, 2011.

Leithart, Peter J. *Heroes of the City of Man: A Christian Guide to Select Ancient Literature.* Moscow, ID: Canon Press, 1999.

Martin, Thomas R. *Ancient Greece: From Prehistoric to Hellenistic Times.* New Haven, CT: Yale UP, 2000.

Otis, Brooks. *Virgil: A Study in Civilized Poetry.* Oxford: Clarendon Press, 1964.

Richards, I. A. *The Philosophy of Rhetoric.* New York: Oxford UP, 1936.

Russo, Joseph. "Homer's Style: Nonformulaic Features of an Oral Aesthetic." *Oral Tradition 9.2* (1994): 371–389. < http://journal.oraltradition.org/files/articles/9ii/10_russo.pdf>

Tyrrell, Robert Y. *Latin Poetry: Lectures Delivered in 1893.* Boston: Houghton, Mifflin, and Co., 1895. <http://books.google.com/books?id=h5wwAAAAYAAJ>

Wiles, David. *Greek Theatre Performance: An Introduction.* Cambridge: Cambridge University Press, 2000.

Bibliography

Abbott, Frank Frost. *A Short History of Rome*. Chicago: Scott, Foresman, and Company, 1906.

Gardiner, Cynthia P. *The Sophoclean Chorus: A Study of Character and Function*. Iowa City: U. of Iowa, 1987.

Hesiod. *Theogony; and Works and Days*. Trans. M. L. West. Oxford: Oxford UP, 2008.

Highet, Gilbert. *Poets in a Landscape*. New York: Alfred A. Knopf, 1965.

Homer. *The Iliad*. Trans. Robert Fitzgerald. Garden City, NY: Anchor/Doubleday, 1974.

---. *The Odyssey*. Trans. Robert Fagles. London: Penguin, 1997.

Leithart, Peter J. *Heroes of the City of Man: A Christian Guide to Select Ancient Literature*. Moscow, ID: Canon Press, 1999.

Martin, Thomas R. *Ancient Greece: From Prehistoric to Hellenistic Times*. New Haven, CT: Yale UP, 2000.

Otis, Brooks. *Virgil: A Study in Civilized Poetry*. Oxford: Clarendon Press, 1964.

Russo, Joseph. "Homer's Style: Nonformulaic Features of an Oral Aesthetic." *Oral Tradition* 9.2 (1994): 371-389. < http://journal.oraltradition.org/files/articles/9ii/10_russo.pdf>

Sophocles. *Oedipus Rex*. Trans. George Young. New York: Dover Publications, 1991.

Tyrrell, Robert Y. *Latin Poetry: Lectures Delivered in 1893*. Boston: Houghton, Mifflin, and Co., 1895. <http://books.google.com/books?id=h5wwAAAAYAAJ>

Virgil. *The Aeneid*. Trans. Robert Fitzgerald. New York, NY: Vintage, 1983.

Wiles, David. *Greek Theatre Performance: An Introduction*. Cambridge: Cambridge, 2000.

EXAMPLES FROM THE

Bible

Examples from the Bible

The common expression that uses "black and white" to distinguish truth from opinion actually does a disservice to the idea of truth. If all truth is God's truth and finds its ultimate expression in His character, then a more accurate description would be to say that truth is like white light—it encompasses all of the beautiful colors we see around us.

In this way, truth and beauty are complementary rather than competitive. Nowhere is this statement more evident than in the literary features of the Bible. Why should we be surprised that a God who created the stars and used the rainbow to symbolize His promises should give to human speech the potential for more than stark, bare communication? Recognizing the lovely poetic features of the Bible enriches our understanding of its message, just as using a prism to diffract white light into its full spectrum of colors enhances our appreciation for light itself.[1]

Every language has its own set of poetic conventions, some of which are difficult to represent in translation. One example is the Hebrew **acrostic** form seen in Psalm 119. Each stanza begins with a subsequent letter of the Hebrew alphabet. Where the English translation of verse one reads, "Blessed are they whose ways are blameless, who walk according to the law of the LORD," the Hebrew transliteration is, "'ašrê təmîmê- dārek; hahōləkîm, bətōwrat Yahweh."[2] The first word begins with the first letter of the Hebrew alphabet, *aleph*. The next stanza (beginning in verse 9) begins with the Hebrew letter *beth*.

Every language is also intertwined with the culture of the people who speak it. For example, Latin uses many war-related metaphors and has multiple words for "wound" and "fight" because the Roman Empire was a military society. Likewise, the colloquial English expression, "Life is simpler if you plow around the stump," would mean more to an agrarian community than it would to an industrial one. Some of the nuances of language get lost or muted in translation—all the more reason to study multiple languages, ancient and modern! Nonetheless, we can still gain a sense of the beauty in biblical language by studying it in translation.

Reading a passage in multiple translations may give you an even richer understanding of the material.

Unless otherwise noted, all Scripture verses used here are taken from the 1984 edition of the New International Version.[3]

Alliteration

- Jeremiah 51:37, "Babylon will be a <u>h</u>eap of ruins,
    a <u>h</u>aunt of jackals,
  an object of <u>h</u>orror and scorn,
    a place where no one lives."

This is an example in which alliteration exists in the English translation as well as in the Hebrew. Notice the repeated use of the consonant "h."

- Psalm 122:6–7, "<u>P</u>ray for the <u>p</u>eace of Jerusalem:
    'May those who love you be secure.
  May there be peace <u>w</u>ithin your <u>w</u>alls
    and <u>s</u>ecurity within your <u>c</u>itadels.'"

Here, the translators have attempted to preserve some of the passage's alliteration. Notice the repeated use of the consonant sound "p" in the first line, "w" in the third, and "s/c" in the fourth. The alliteration is much more prominent in the Hebrew, which reads,

---

1 Did you notice the simile? You can tell it is a simile and not a metaphor because the word "as" makes the comparison explicit.
2 *The Interlinear Bible*. Glassport, PA: The Online Parallel Bible Project, 2011, Web. Accessed 09/04/12 from http://interlinearbible.org. Transliterations have been reversed so they read left-to-right instead of right-to-left, as in the original Hebrew.
3 THE HOLY BIBLE, NEW INTERNATIONAL VERSION®, NIV® Copyright © 1984 by International Bible Society. Used by permission of Zondervan. All rights reserved.

"ălū šəlōwm yərūšālim;
yišlāyū, 'ōhăḇāyiḵ.
yəhî- šālōwm bəḥêlêḵ;
ləwāh, bə'armənōwṯāyiḵ."

Some types of alliteration create a harsh sound, but other repeated consonants give the poem a soothing tone when it is read aloud. (Note: The underscoring in this example is part of the Hebrew transliteration.)

Allusion

- John 8:58–59, "'I tell you the truth,' Jesus answered, '<u>before Abraham was born, I am</u>!' At this, they picked up stones to stone him, but Jesus hid himself, slipping away from the temple grounds."

Scholars speculate that the Jews attempted to stone Jesus at this moment because he was identifying himself with the name of God by alluding to Exodus 3:14, in which God tells Moses, "I AM WHO I AM. This is what you are to say to the Israelites: 'I AM has sent me to you.'"

Anaphora

- Amos 3:3–5, "<u>Do</u> two walk together
    unless they have agreed to do so?
  <u>Does</u> a lion roar in the thicket
    when he has no prey?
  <u>Does</u> he growl in his den
    when he has caught nothing?
  <u>Does</u> a bird fall into a trap on the ground
    where no snare has been set?
  <u>Does</u> a trap spring up from the earth
    when there is nothing to catch?"

Anaphora is a form of parallelism, as you can see in this example from the book of Amos. Each line takes the form of a question, and more specifically, each sentence begins with the same auxiliary verb, "do" or "does." The second line of each couplet also demonstrates anaphora. Each one is an adverbial clause, and most of them begin with the word "when."

- Micah 6:15, "<u>You will</u> plant but not harvest;
    <u>you will</u> press olives but not use the oil on yourselves,
    <u>you will</u> crush grapes but not drink the wine."

Repeating the same structure but using different examples each time allows the prophet to emphasize his point through repetition. In case his audience did not grasp the weight of his message the first time, he piles on more and more examples to ensure that they understand.

Antithesis

- Genesis 4:4–5, "<u>The LORD looked with favor on Abel and his offering, but on Cain and his offering he did not look with favor</u>."

The basic structure of the two clauses is parallel, but the verb is opposite: the Lord looked, on one hand, and he did not look, on the other. The structure of this sentence calls attention to the stark contrast between Cain and Abel. They are closely linked, but also very different in their relationship to God.

- Job 1:21, "<u>Naked I came</u> from my mother's womb, <u>and naked I will depart. The LORD gave</u> and <u>the LORD has taken away</u>."

Job acknowledges that God's sovereignty is absolute at both ends of his life, birth and death. As a result, God has the right to bless Job and to try him.

Apostrophe

- Genesis 9:25, "He said, '<u>Cursed be Canaan!</u>
    The lowest of slaves
    will he be to his brothers.'"

Canaan is the name given to Ham's descendants. When Noah curses Canaan, he speaks as though the nation that would derive from Ham's descendants were standing in front of him along with Ham.

Assonance

- Lamentations 2:6, "He has l<u>ai</u>d w<u>a</u>ste his dwelling
    like a garden;
    he has destroyed his pl<u>a</u>ce of meeting."

In this passage, the English translation shows an example of assonance in the repeated vowel sound of a long "a."

- Proverbs 13:20, "He who walks with the wise grows wise,
    but a companion of fools suffers harm."

This is a good example of a passage in which the assonance is not readily apparent in translation. The Hebrew words "w'roeh" and "yërôa" repeat several vowel sounds, but the English translations—"companion" and "suffers harm"—do not.

Examples from the Bible

Asyndeton

- 1 Thessalonians. 5:19–22, "<u>Do not put out</u> the Spirit's fire; <u>do not treat</u> prophecies with contempt. <u>Test</u> everything. <u>Hold</u> on to the good. <u>Avoid</u> every kind of evil."

Formal rhetoric uses the term "asyndeton" specifically when grammatically necessary conjunctions are left out of a sentence. A broader definition often includes parallel sentences that are not joined together by connecting words, as in the example above. The effect of asyndeton is similar to a staccato rhythm in music; each note (sentence, clause) jabs the reader individually, demanding attention.

Chiasmus

- Genesis 1:27, "So <u>God created man in his own image</u>,
    <u>in the image of God he created him</u>."

The first clause has subject (God) + verb (created) + direct object (man) + prepositional phrase modifying the verb (in his own image). In the second clause, the structure is reversed; the prepositional phrase comes first. God's act of creation is the first and last idea in the sentence, and the fact that man was made in God's image is at the center, repeated for emphasis.

Consonance

- John 1:1–2, "In the beginning was the <u>Word</u>, and the <u>Word</u> was with <u>God</u>, and the <u>Word</u> was <u>God</u>. He was with <u>God</u> in the beginning."

In the English translation, "Word" and "God" demonstrate consonance because both end with the consonant "d," but the preceding vowel sounds differ slightly.

Epistrophe

- Genesis 1:5, 8, 13, 19, 23, and 31, "<u>And there was evening, and there was morning—the [–th] day</u>."

The orderly sequence of creation is reinforced by the fact that each day ends with the same refrain.

Foreshadowing

- Matthew 26:10–12 (KJV), "When Jesus understood it, he said unto them, Why trouble ye the woman? for she hath wrought a good work upon me. For ye

have the poor always with you; but <u>me ye have not always</u>. For in that she hath poured this ointment on my body, she did it for my burial."

Jesus foretells his death many times to his disciples, sometimes explicitly and sometimes more subtly, as in the underlined example of foreshadowing. Like the disciples, we, too, may be slow to understand and believe the meaning of His words.

Hyperbole

- Matthew 23:24, "You blind guides! <u>You strain out a gnat but swallow a camel</u>."

As Jesus reprimands the Pharisees, his point is not literally that they have indigestion because they have been eating camels. Rather, he is giving an example to show that they overemphasize the details of the law and miss its spirit. He makes the same argument in the previous verse when he explains that they tithe precisely and yet they neglect to show mercy to those around them. The use of hyperbole shows the Pharisees how ludicrous their principles appear when they are applied to other situations.

- Deuteronomy 1:28, "Where can we go? Our brothers have made us lose heart. They say, 'The people are stronger and taller than we are; the cities are large, <u>with walls up to the sky</u>.'"

When the first Israelite spies entered the Promised Land, they returned full of fear. The walls of the cities they saw had been built by men and could not be tall enough to break through the earth's atmosphere, yet to the terrified spies, this hyperbole seemed true.

Imagery

- Luke 23:44–45, " It was now about the sixth hour, and darkness came over the whole land until the ninth hour, for the sun stopped shining."

As Jesus dies on the cross, even things that most humans would consider fixed and wholly natural (the division of the world into regular cycles of light and darkness) break down, becoming images of the disruption that is taking place in the spiritual world.

Litotes

- 2 Corinthians 2:10–11, "If you forgive anyone, I also forgive him. And what I have forgiven—if there was anything to forgive—I have forgiven in the sight of Christ for your sake, in order that Satan might not outwit us. For we are not unaware of his schemes."

The direct form of this statement would be, "We are aware of his schemes." By using litotes, Paul refutes any attempt by members of the church to plead ignorance in this matter.

- Hebrews 6:10, "God is not unjust; he will not forget your work and the love you have shown him as you have helped his people and continue to help them."

Likewise, the author of Hebrews could have written simply, "God is just." By using this type of indirect statement, he leaves that conclusion for his readers to draw. He also reassures them, recognizing that some of his readers might believe the lie that God is unjust. In this way, the rhetorical device matches the tone of the previous verse, which encourages the Hebrews, "Even though we speak like this, dear friends, we are confident of better things in your case—things that accompany salvation" (v. 9).

Metaphor

- Job 1:9–10, "'Does Job fear God for nothing?' Satan replied. 'Have you not put a hedge around him and his household and everything he has?'"

Satan is not suggesting that God has literally planted a wall of shrubbery around Job's home. He is comparing God's protection to a hedge. Just as a hedge would guard the animals or people contained within it, so also God is defending Job.

- Job 4:8, "As I have observed, those who plow evil and those who sow trouble reap it."

Eliphaz is not suggesting that evil is a type of soil or that trouble comes in seed form. He is comparing the work of a farmer to the consequences of one's actions. Just as a farmer harvests wheat because he planted wheat seeds instead of corn, so too a man who faces hard times must have done something to deserve them. (Job later refutes this argument.)

Metonymy

- Genesis 3:7, "Then the eyes of both of them were opened, and they realized they were naked; so they sewed fig leaves together and made coverings for themselves."

Adam and Eve were not necessarily walking around with their eyes closed before this time. Imagine when you want to surprise someone with a gift. You might instruct him to keep his eyes closed while you bring the gift in and set it in front of him. "Opening the eyes" is closely associated with discovery or realization, so this verse uses the image to stand in for Adam and Eve's new self-consciousness.

Onomatopoeia

- Job 4:10, "The lions may roar and growl, yet the teeth of the great lions are broken."

The pronunciation of the words "roar" and "growl" is very similar to the sounds they represent. When you read this verse, you can almost hear the threatening noises of the lions, and yet Eliphaz claims that their ferocity is nothing compared to God's.

- Genesis 1:2, "Now the earth was formless and empty, darkness was over the surface of the deep, and the Spirit of God was hovering over the waters."

Because onomatopoeia is so specific to its language of origin, it is difficult to replicate in translation. Genesis 1:2 is often used as an example because the Hebrew phrase "tohû wävohû," which means "formless and empty," has a disordered, chaotic sound that the English translation does not.

Parallelism

- Genesis 1:3–5, "<u>And God said, 'Let there be light,'</u> <u>and there was light</u>. <u>God saw that the light was good</u>, and he separated the light from the darkness. <u>God called</u> the light 'day,' and the darkness he called 'night.' <u>And there was evening, and there was morning —the first day</u>."

Each day of creation follows a similar pattern: God said. God named. And God saw that it was good. As a result, day six, the day on which God created man, stands out from the rest: on this day, God broke the pattern. He said not just that it was good, but that "it was very good" (v. 31).

Personification

- Genesis 4:10–11, "The LORD said, 'What have you done? Listen! <u>Your brother's blood cries out</u> to me from the ground. Now you are under a curse and driven from the ground, <u>which opened its mouth</u> to receive your brother's blood from your hand.'"

Blood has neither a mouth nor vocal chords with which to cry out, but God talks about Abel's blood as though it were a person. Likewise, the ground can absorb blood, but God gives it the human feature of a mouth in order to make his point more emphatically to Cain.

Polysyndeton

- Haggai 1:11, "I called for a drought on the fields <u>and</u> the mountains, on the grain, the new wine, the oil <u>and</u> whatever the ground produces, on men and cattle, <u>and</u> on the labor of your hands."

From a grammatical perspective, this list could be simplified: "I called for a drought on the fields, the mountains, the grain, the new wine, the oil, whatever the ground produces, men, cattle, and the labor of your hands." Stretching out this list by using polysyndeton highlights the devastating extent of the Lord's judgment.

- Acts 1:8, "But you will receive power when the Holy Spirit comes on you; and you will be my witnesses in Jerusalem, <u>and</u> in all Judea and Samaria, <u>and</u> to the ends of the earth."

As widespread as God's judgment is in the passage from Haggai, his compassion and good news are equally far-reaching. In this passage, polysyndeton says to the reader, "Wait—there is more! The disciples will also be witnesses in Judea and Samaria. Wait—I'm not done yet! They will also be disciples to the ends of the earth."

Rhyme

- Proverbs 11:2, "<u>When pride comes, then comes disgrace,</u>
    but with humility comes wisdom."

Rhyme is less common than other literary devices in biblical poetry, and like alliteration and assonance, it is often lost in translation. In this proverb, the Hebrew words "Bä-zädôn" and "qälôn" rhyme, but the English translations "pride" and "disgrace" do not.

Simile

- Job 3:24, "For sighing comes to me instead of food;
    <u>my groans pour out like water</u>."

Job explicitly compares the way groans emerge from his mouth to the way water pours out of a vessel. If you have ever seen water poured out of a jar, you know that it flows smoothly and without ceasing until the jar is empty or until the person pouring it sets it upright. Job is saying that there are no discernable breaks between his groans; they flow out steadily and as naturally as water does.

- Psalm 1:3, "<u>He is like a tree</u> planted by streams of water,
    which yields its fruit in season
and whose leaf does not wither.
    Whatever he does prospers."

The psalmist could have simply said, "Whatever he does prospers," but to make the statement richer, he explicitly compares the man who delights in God's law to a tree planted near a source of water. Both of them have a ready source of sustenance, so they are able to flourish.

Synecdoche

- Job 4:4, "Your words have supported those who stumbled;
    <u>you have strengthened faltering knees</u>."

Job is saying that God has strengthened people who became weary, but instead of saying that, he picks a relevant, specific part of those people to stand in for the whole. When someone is weak, you might notice his knees trembling, so Job says, "you have strengthened faltering knees" as a more colorful way to say, "you have strengthened weary people."

For Further Reading

Gray, George Buchanan. *The Forms of Hebrew Poetry*. London: Hoddard and Stoughton, 1915.

Harmon, William, and Hugh Holman. *A Handbook to Literature*. 10th ed. Upper Saddle River, NJ: Pearson/Prentice Hall, 2006.

Kern, Andrew. *The Lost Tools of Writing: Level 1*. 4th ed. Concord, NC: The CiRCE Institute, 2011.

The Interlinear Bible. Glassport, PA: The Online Parallel Bible Project, 2011.